The
California
Seafood
Cookbook

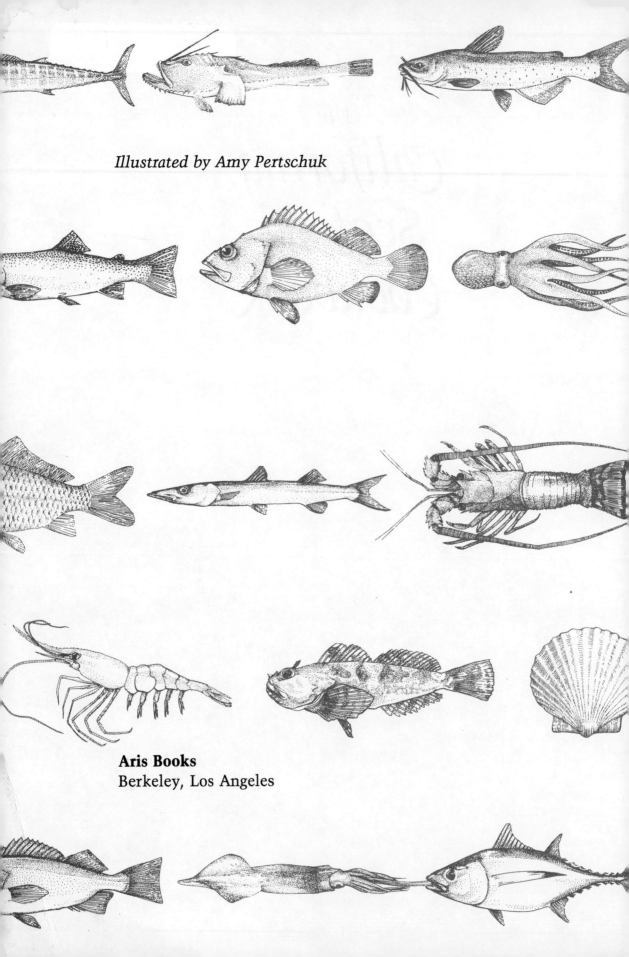

Illustrated by Amy Pertschuk

Aris Books
Berkeley, Los Angeles

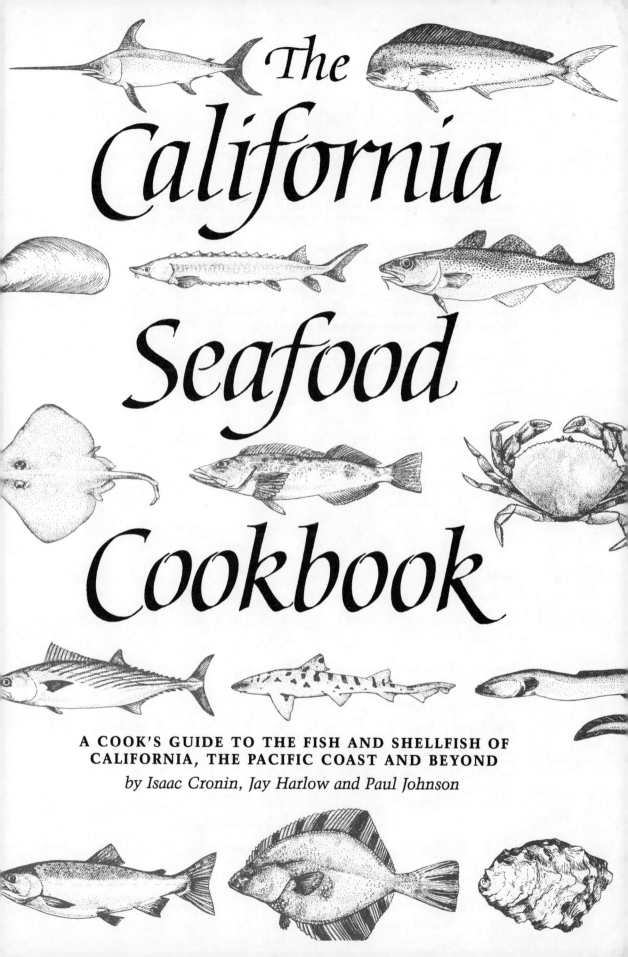

The California Seafood Cookbook

A COOK'S GUIDE TO THE FISH AND SHELLFISH OF CALIFORNIA, THE PACIFIC COAST AND BEYOND

by Isaac Cronin, Jay Harlow and Paul Johnson

Conceived and produced by L. John Harris
Edited by Sidney Weinstein, Deborah Bruner, Tim Ware and L. John Harris
Book and cover design by Jeanne Jambu
The book was set in Trump by Linda Davis of Ann Flanagan Typography
Calligraphy by John Prestianni.
The book was printed and bound by Maple-Vail Book Manufacturing.
The binding on this book has been Smyth sewn for strength and easy opening.

Aris Books are published by
Harris Publishing Company, Inc.
1635 Channing Way
Berkeley, CA 94703

Library of Congress Cataloging in Publication Data

Cronin, Isaac, 1948–
California Seafood Cookbook.

Bibliography: p. 283
Includes index.
1. Cookery (Seafood)   2. Seafood.   I. Harlow, Jay, 1953–
II. Johnson, Paul, 1948–   III. Title.
TX747.c84 1983   641.6'9   82-24450
ISBN 0-943186-04-8
ISBN 0-943186-03-X (pbk.)

Manufactured in the United States of America
6 8 9 7
First printing January 1983

CONTENTS

Illustrated Species Index

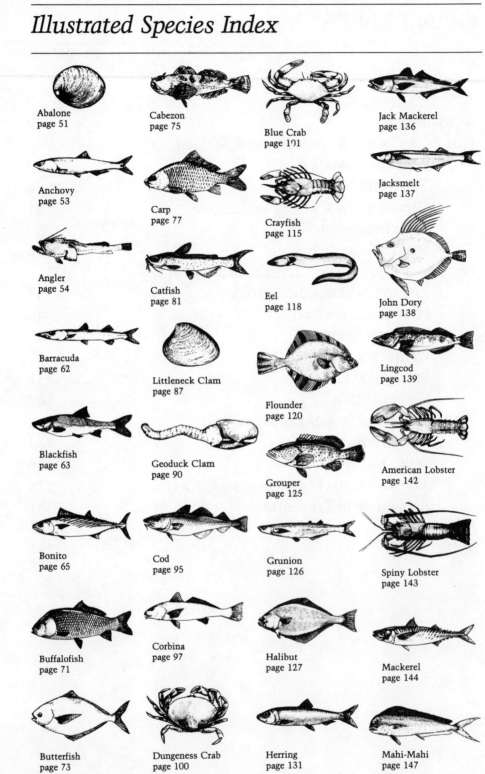

Abalone
page 51

Cabezon
page 75

Blue Crab
page 101

Jack Mackerel
page 136

Anchovy
page 53

Carp
page 77

Crayfish
page 115

Jacksmelt
page 137

Angler
page 54

Catfish
page 81

Eel
page 118

John Dory
page 138

Barracuda
page 62

Littleneck Clam
page 87

Flounder
page 120

Lingcod
page 139

Blackfish
page 63

Geoduck Clam
page 90

Grouper
page 125

American Lobster
page 142

Bonito
page 65

Cod
page 95

Grunion
page 126

Spiny Lobster
page 143

Buffalofish
page 71

Corbina
page 97

Halibut
page 127

Mackerel
page 144

Butterfish
page 73

Dungeness Crab
page 100

Herring
page 131

Mahi-Mahi
page 147

7

Mussel
page 148

Octopus
page 154

Oyster
page 156

Periwinkle
page 167

Redfish
page 168

Red Snapper
page 169

Rockfish (Bolina)
page 171

Rockfish (Goldeneye)
page 171

Rockfish (Yellowtail)
page 172

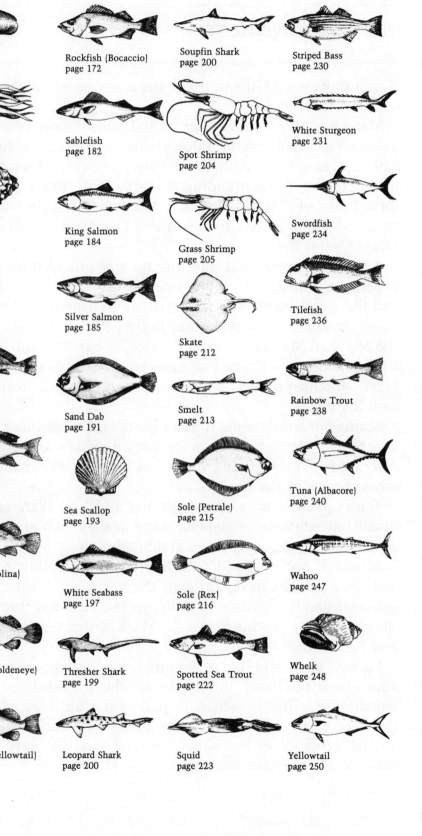

Rockfish (Bocaccio)
page 172

Sablefish
page 182

King Salmon
page 184

Silver Salmon
page 185

Sand Dab
page 191

Sea Scallop
page 193

White Seabass
page 197

Thresher Shark
page 199

Leopard Shark
page 200

Soupfin Shark
page 200

Spot Shrimp
page 204

Grass Shrimp
page 205

Skate
page 212

Smelt
page 213

Sole (Petrale)
page 215

Sole (Rex)
page 216

Spotted Sea Trout
page 222

Squid
page 223

Striped Bass
page 230

White Sturgeon
page 231

Swordfish
page 234

Tilefish
page 236

Rainbow Trout
page 238

Tuna (Albacore)
page 240

Wahoo
page 247

Whelk
page 248

Yellowtail
page 250

Acknowledgements

The authors would like to thank the many people who contributed to this book.

Many Bay Area restaurant chefs and other talented cooks provided recipes and specific information on culinary techniques. These include Bruce Aidells of Poulet, Somchai Aksomboon of Siam Cuisine, Carol Brendlinger of Bay Wolf, Bruce Cost, Victoria Fahey of Curds and Whey, William Marinelli, Jeremiah Tower of Santa Fe Bar and Grill and Dan Wormhoudt of Gulf Coast Oyster Bar.

A wealth of technical information was provided by various experts including many wholesale fish dealers of San Francisco and the Bay Area: Tony Porti, William Marinelli and the West Coast Aquaculture Foundation; Robert Pata and Joe Farrell of the National Marine Fisheries Service; Robert Price and Fred S. Conte of the Sea Grant Program, University of California at Davis; and Joan Eesley and Larry Marsali of the California Seafood Institute.

Seeing our words come to life through the magnificent drawings of Amy Pertschuk was a joy and an inspiration. We thank Amy for patiently bearing with us as we kept adding more and more species to the book.

Sidney Weinstein, Deborah Bruner and Tim Ware supplied invaluable editorial assistance, and Jeanne Jambu imparted clarity and elegance with her graphic design.

Although not involved in this project, the following chefs and restaurateurs have, through the years, provided culinary guidance and inspiration, and their presence is felt throughout the book: Anne Powning Haskell, Mark Miller, Jeremiah Tower and Patty Unterman.

Finally, we would like to acknowledge the support and guidance of our publisher, John Harris, who provided us with a wonderful facility in which to pursue our culinary interests, the freedom to define and organize this book according to the special demands of the subject matter, and his enthusiastic appetite at our recipe testings.

Introduction

In the fall of 1981, John Harris, our publisher, approached the three of us with an idea for a California seafood cookbook. Each of us—a food writer, a restaurant chef and a fishmonger—agreed on the need for a comprehensive culinary guide to the variety of seafood available in California. We had found that most seafood cookbooks, while they may have excellent recipes, are written from an Atlantic or Gulf Coast perspective; with very few exceptions, Pacific species are given at best passing mention. Cooks on the West Coast have had to fend for themselves in adapting Eastern recipes to locally available fish.

As we began to catalogue the varieties of seafood available in California, it became clear that we also wanted to capture the spirit of an eclectic, adventurous style of cookery which is typically Californian. Using the finest and freshest ingredients available and incorporating a wide range of ethnic influences, the chefs, caterers and cooking teachers of the Bay Area are among the best exponents of this style. Several of them came to our test kitchen during the development of this book, demonstrating techniques and contributing recipes.

However strong our enthusiasm might be for this California approach to seafood, our work would be of little use to cooks in other parts of the country if we limited ourselves entirely to local species. To avoid our own form of provincialism, we decided to test as many Atlantic and Gulf species as we could obtain, to determine which could serve as alternatives for the Pacific varieties featured in our recipes.

The California Seafood Cookbook, then, is a comprehensive guide to identifying, buying, cleaning, cutting, cooking and serving seafood available on the Pacific Coast. Part I, "A Cook's Introduction to Seafood," presents the preliminaries to cooking: techniques for judging freshness, step-by-step cleaning and cutting procedures, cooking methods and special ingredients. The heart of the book is Part II, "A Cook's Encyclopedia of Seafood." The emphasis is on species available here, whether from local waters or brought in by air, sometimes

literally from around the world. Each variety is carefully illustrated so that the book can serve as a "field guide" to fish in
the market.

An important feature of the recipes in the encyclopedia is the
listing of alternative species, including Pacific, Atlantic and
Gulf varieties. Cooks in California, for example, will find that
the recipe for Sautéed Corbina with Piquant Sauce on page 98
will work equally well with some other local species such as
white seabass; readers in Louisiana are advised to try it with
their own redfish, and New Yorkers may freely substitute
striped bass.

The recipes in this book are a personal selection and reflect
many, but by no means all, of the ethnic styles to be found in
California kitchens. They tend toward simple approaches to a
limited number of ingredients rather than elaborate creations;
they are intended to show off the food, not the cook. Because
they rely on fresh, seasonal ingredients, which may not always
be available, they encourage flexibility and improvisation. They
draw on many cultural and culinary traditions, but are not
bound to any one way of doing things. In short, they represent
the way many Californians cook and eat.

We hope that our readers, in California and elsewhere, will
use *The California Seafood Cookbook* in the spirit in which it
was written. Researching and writing this book was a wonderful learning experience for us. There were a few disappoint-
ments along the way, but many more pleasant surprises. We
hope that you will find this book useful in your own discovery
of the pleasures of seafood cookery.

—Isaac Cronin, Jay Harlow,
Paul Johnson

Berkeley, California

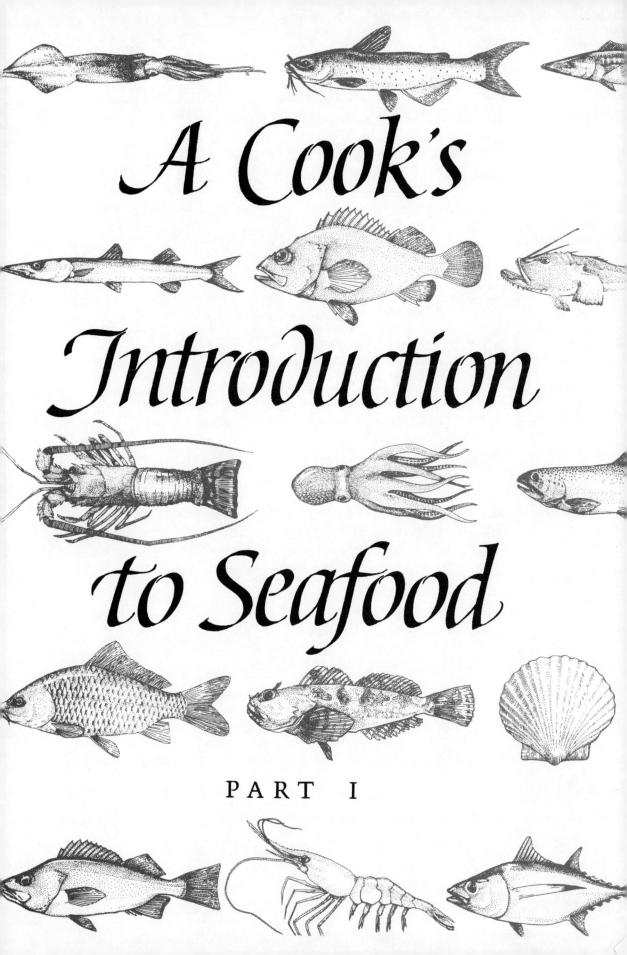

A Cook's Introduction to Seafood

PART I

AT THE FISH MARKET
A GUIDE TO BUYING FRESH SEAFOOD

S EAFOOD spoils most quickly of all foods. From the moment a fish leaves the water, bacteria which are abundant in the aquatic environment begin to break down the flesh. Cold temperatures retard this process, but even under optimal conditions seafood should be used as quickly as possible after it is caught.

The quality of seafood depends not only on how long it has been out of the water, but also on how it is handled. Certain fishing methods are rougher on seafood, rendering it more perishable. Some fishermen are very conscientious about careful

Available Forms

ROUND: The whole fish, as it comes out of the water (applies equally to flatfish)

DRESSED: Entrails removed, head intact, gills may or may not be removed

PAN-DRESSED: Dressed, head and scales removed, fins and tail may be trimmed

BLOCK: A section of a large dressed fish (primarily shark and swordfish) cut across, including skin and bone

CHUNK: An equivalent piece of a smaller fish, such as a whole salmon tail

STEAK: (a) A slice up to 2 inches thick through the body of a dressed fish, including skin and bone (salmon, seabass, halibut, etc.) (b) A slice of similar thickness, perpendicular to the bone, of a quarter or other section of a large fish (shark, swordfish, tuna), often skinless

FILET: The boneless meat of one side of a fish removed in one piece, with or without the skin; also pieces cut from a large filet or boneless meat in general

FLETCHES: Half-filets of halibut or other large flatfish, made by separating the whole filet along the seam parallel to the backbone

SLICES: Sections of a large filet or fletch (salmon, seabass, lingcod, halibut, etc.), cut diagonally or perpendicular to the bone. Usually, thicker pieces yield one per serving

SCALLOPS: Same as slices but usually thinner, two or more per serving

14 handling and immediate icing of their catch; others are not. Wholesalers also vary in their care of and attention to quality of their product, and retailers may mix several catches in the same batch.

With all these variables, the cook must learn to shop carefully, evaluating each fish on its own merits. Do not assume that all the fish at a given market, or even all the fish of a given species, are of the same quality. If at all possible, buy round (whole) fish (see Available Forms, page 13). It is easiest to judge the quality of fish in this form, and the head, bones and trimmings can be used for stocks. Most fishmongers will clean round fish for little or no charge if you do not wish to clean it yourself.

Selecting Seafood

Keep the following rules in mind when choosing seafood in the market:

Be flexible. It is best to go to the market with a cooking method or a general approach rather than a particular fish in mind.

Eat what is in season. This rule more than any other will insure that you are getting the best seafood available as well as the best value. Don't insist on having grilled swordfish during the height of salmon season.

Buy fish the same day you plan to cook it. Very fresh seafood will keep another day, but the quality will certainly deteriorate.

Ask the fishmonger for recommendations. After all, it is his job to know what is best. If you feel, however, that a fishmonger has recommended something because he wants to get rid of it, try another fish market.

Don't be afraid to ask for special services such as having a crab cleaned or a fish boned for stuffing. Be prepared to pay for these extras, which take time.

When placing special orders, be prepared to leave a deposit, especially if your request is at all unusual. Again, be flexible, and allow for the possibility that the fish you want may not be available on the day you want it.

Judging Freshness

The following are guidelines for judging the freshness of fish and shellfish. Important exceptions to the rules are given in parentheses.

ROUND FISH

Flesh should be firm or elastic to the touch, even to the point of *rigor mortis.* (Some fish may be so fresh that *rigor mortis* will not have set in yet.)

Odor should be clean and pleasant, like brine or fresh water, with no "fishy" smell around the gills. (Shark and skate sometimes have an ammonia smell, which should disappear with acidulation.)

Gills should be bright pink or red. (Gills of some flatfish may be darkened by mud depending upon how they were caught, but should be bright red when washed.)

Eyes should be clear and protruding. (Eyes of some deep-water fish, such as rockfish and grouper, may be cloudy due to pressure changes as they are raised from the bottom.)

Skin should be brightly colored, with scales tightly attached.

FILETS AND STEAKS

Although there are many fewer clues to freshness once a fish has been cut up, some of the above guidelines apply. Filets or steaks should have a bright, moist appearance, with no brown, yellow or pink discoloration, and a clean, fresh odor.

LIVE FISH

Freshwater species such as catfish, buffalofish, blackfish and eel are often kept alive in tanks. Choose only lively specimens.

16   SHELLFISH

From a cook's standpoint, shellfish fall into three main categories: crustaceans (crab, lobster, shrimp, crayfish); cephalopods (squid, octopus); and molluscs (including bivalves—clams, mussels, oysters, scallops—and univalves—abalone, whelk, periwinkles). As with fish, a clean, fresh aroma is a good indication of quality. The following are guidelines for each category:

Crustaceans

Live crustaceans should be lively, and seem heavy for their size. Shrimp, which are generally not sold alive, should have their heads firmly attached, with no blackening of the gill area just behind the head. It is not true that once a crab or lobster dies, it must be immediately discarded; it should, however, be cleaned and iced as soon as possible and cooked the same day.

Cooked crustaceans should have legs, claws and tail (if any) pulled in tightly. This is a sign that they were fresh and alive when cooked.

Cephalopods

Squid and octopus should have ivory flesh under the thin colored skin, with no discolorations.

Molluscs

Live bivalves should have tightly closed shells, or close them quickly when handled. Any which remain open are dead and should be discarded.

Univalves should also be alive, and the exposed muscle should react to the touch. To keep bivalves alive, *do not* store them in water, but keep them refrigerated and covered with a damp cloth. These intertidal species are used to being out of the water, and may keep for up to a week stored this way. (They will, of course, taste better if used promptly.) Oysters are the only bivalves which are generally stored after shucking; they should be kept in covered jars with *clear* liquid, refrigerated.

Freezing Seafood

Unless you catch more than you can use, freezing seafood is not a good idea. The connective fiber (collagen) in seafood is delicate and breaks down quickly in freezing and thawing, causing moisture and flavor loss which no cooking method or recipe can restore. And while freezing slows down spoilage of fish, it does not entirely stop it, especially when freezer temperatures are above 0°, which is the case with most home freezers.

If you must freeze seafood, observe the following guidelines:

Wrap the fish tightly and seal it well. Use a second layer of wrapping to minimize the possibility of direct contact with cold air, which will draw moisture out of the fish.

Use a freezer rather than the freezing compartment of a refrigerator if at all possible. A temperature of not more than 0° is optimal. The quicker the fish is frozen and the more even the temperature remains, the less moisture will be lost from the fish. Generally, shellfish freeze better than fish, and lean fish better than those with a higher fat content.

Thaw frozen seafood in the refrigerator until it reaches refrigerator temperature, and cook it the same day it is thawed. Never refreeze seafood that has been thawed.

TOOLS AND EQUIPMENT

*T*HE *following is not a complete list of kitchen equipment, but rather a catalogue of the kinds of special equipment needed for fish cookery which might not be found in a home kitchen. In some cases, we are merely expressing our personal preferences. What is most important is to know the cooking characteristics of your own equipment—how it handles, how it cooks and its limitations.*

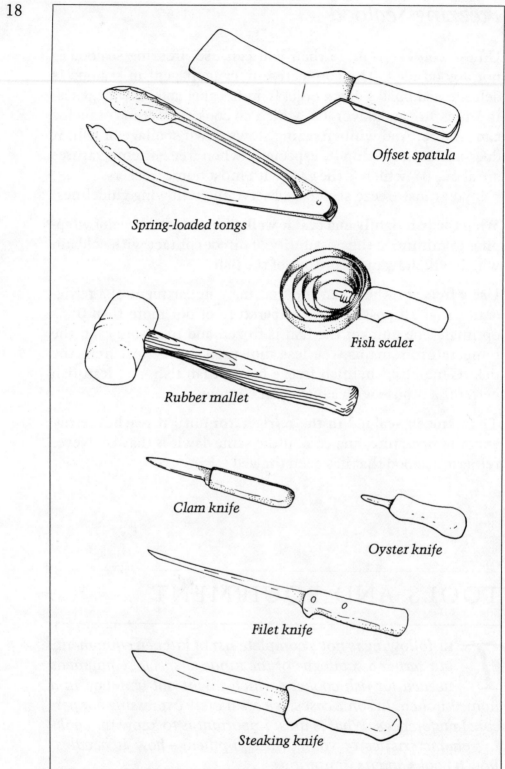

Offset spatula

Spring-loaded tongs

Fish scaler

Rubber mallet

Clam knife

Oyster knife

Filet knife

Steaking knife

Knives

In addition to the basics—*paring knife* and *French chef's knife* or *Chinese cleaver*—one type of knife is virtually indispensable when dealing with whole fish. It is called, appropriately enough, a *filet knife*. The filet knife looks like an elongated *boning knife* with a thin, flexible, tapered blade at least 7 inches long, and preferably up to 9 inches. (If the 9-inch variety is not available through normal retail outlets, try a commercial fisherman's supply store.) This knife allows for the fastest and cleanest fileting of all sizes and shapes of fish. A conventional boning knife will, of course, do the job, but will require more and shorter cuts and will tend to produce rather torn-up looking filets.

While a *Chinese cleaver* is thought of in this country primarily as a vegetable knife, it is a very useful tool for cleaning round fish, as a few minutes spent in a fish market in any Chinatown will amply demonstrate. It is also ideal for splitting fish heads for stock.

Hand Tools

We strongly recommend stocking your kitchen from commercial restaurant supply houses whenever possible. High-tech decor aside, these dealers carry tools of proven design and generally reliable quality, each designed to do a given job efficiently and for a long time. Among the hand tools especially useful for fish cookery are: an *offset spatula* with an 8-inch blade; spring-loaded stainless *tongs*, rather than the scissor-action type; and heat resistant *rubber spatulas* in a variety of sizes. Other specialized tools we found very handy in the development of our recipes are: a *tomato corer*, which looks like a tiny scoop with teeth and deftly removes the stem core; and a *lemon zester*, which removes the flavorful outer peel of citrus fruits, leaving behind the bitter white membrane.

20 *Cookware*

Very little in the way of special cookware is required for the recipes in this book. Except where noted, the material of the cooking surface (cast iron, aluminum, stainless steel, enamel or non-stick coating) is not as important as its cooking characteristics; look for fairly heavy bottoms which spread the heat evenly. Where a recipe calls for a "non-aluminum" pan, use one with a non-reactive surface such as stainless, enamel, non-stick coating or anodized aluminum. Avoid uncoated aluminum, cast iron or copper.

The *wok*, that traditional Chinese masterpiece of cooking design, no longer needs introduction in this country. In addition to its most common use for stir-frying, we found the *wok* ideal for frying and steaming fish and for tossing pasta in sauce. A 14-inch rolled steel, round-bottomed *wok* with a single wooden handle seems to us the most versatile. Complete sets of accessories are widely available, and should include a flat metal perforated tray for steaming and a semi-circular wire rack for draining fried foods.

While no home grilling equipment can quite equal the intense heat of a restaurant charcoal broiler, the same advantages of quick cooking and sealing of the fish juices can be achieved on a variety of grill types. Charcoal is the choice for a heat source, and may be contained in a home barbecue or *hibachi*. The latter provides the most compact form of heat, and can be set up on a porch or even on a windowsill planter box. Unprocessed hardwood charcoal such as *Mexican mesquite* is preferable to charcoal briquets, both in heat output and burning time and flavor.

Various indoor electric grilling systems exist, from tabletop models with rotisserie attachments to built-in stove-top grills with cast-iron artificial coals and exhaust fans. We tested several of our grilled fish recipes on the latter and found it to produce an agreeable dish, but considerably more slowly and lacking the distinctive flavor of charcoal smoke.

CLEANING AND CUTTING TECHNIQUES

*T*HE *following pages contain techniques which apply to a number of species. Special techniques particular to one species are described along with the fish's entry in the encyclopedia, Part II.*

Typical Bone Structure of Round-bodied Fish*

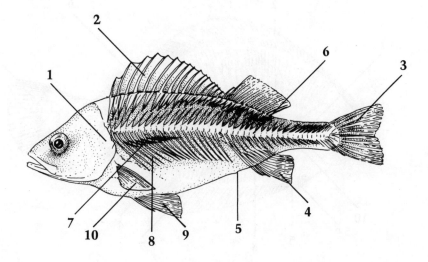

1. **Operculum or gill cover**	6. **Backbone (spine)**
2. **Dorsal fin**	7. **Pin bones (7)**
3. **Tail or caudal fin**	8. **Ribs**
4. **Anal fin**	9. **Pelvic fin (2)**
5. **Vent**	10. **Pectoral fin (2)**

"Round-bodied" refers to one of two basic body shapes. "Round" is a professional term used for whole, undressed fish (see page 13).

22   *Familiarize yourself with the general bone structure of the two basic fish types—round-bodied and flat—before starting to work. Many of the instructions use anatomical terms to avoid confusion, e.g. "dorsal" instead of "back" or "top."*

Important: Make as few cuts as possible, especially when fileting, and try to cut with long, smooth strokes. Professional cutters do this not only for the sake of speed, but to yield filets with smooth surfaces.

Typical Bone Structure of Flat Fish

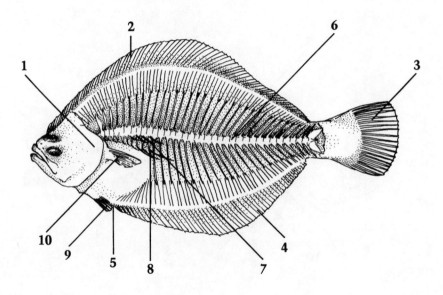

1. Operculum or gill cover	6. Backbone (spine)
2. Dorsal fin	7. Pin bones (7)
3. Tail or caudal fin	8. Ribs
4. Anal fin	9. Pelvic fin (2)
5. Vent	10. Pectoral fin (2)

Fileting a Round-bodied Fish

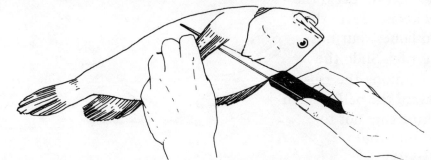

1 Place the fish on its side, dorsal fin toward you and head toward your cutting hand. Lift the pectoral fin and cut diagonally just behind the operculum toward the head. (Note that the filet extends well up into the head.) Be careful not to pierce the entrails at the belly end of the cut.

2 At the end of the first stroke, twist the knife until the edge is facing the tail and the point rests against the spine.

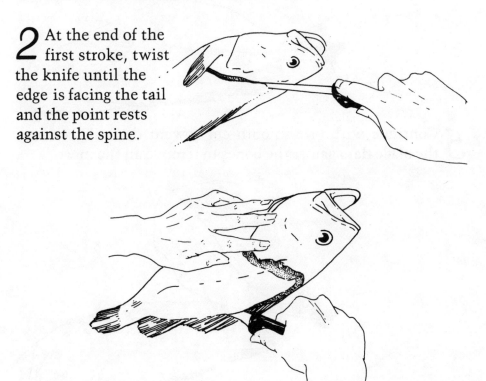

3 Probe with the tip of the knife for the backbone. Holding the blade horizontally, slide the knife along the ribs toward the tail, scraping along the bones to cut away the back side of the filet.

24

4 Gently peel back the filet to reveal the backbone. Sever the pin bones, but not the ribs. Slide the knife along the ribs toward the belly, again taking care not to cut into the entrails.

5 Continue with one smooth cut toward the tail, bending the blade flat against the bones to remove all the meat.

6 Pull the filet free and sever the skin along the anal fin. Turn the fish over, with the belly still facing away from you and the head in the opposite direction. Repeat the above steps for the other filet.

Fileting a Flatfish

Flatfish may be fileted by essentially the same process as above. Large flatfish are actually easier to filet than most round-bodied fish, as the belly cavity is more compact and the filets are larger. Halibut or other large species may also be cut into fletches by first cutting through the filet to the backbone along the lateral line, then cutting away each half filet from the bone.

Skinning Filets

Unless a recipe specifies filets with the skin on, filets should be skinned. Place the filet skin side down on the board. Hold the tail end of the skin down with a fingernail and make a shallow cut under the filet to the skin. Holding the knife at about a 10–15° angle to the board, scrape along the skin without cutting through it. Hold the skin taut and try to make one long, smooth cut. Remove the strips of soft flesh close to the fins, either by hand or with the knife.

Scaling a Fish

If a fish is to be cooked with the skin on, it is generally scaled before dressing. (Fish without scales, such as flounder and bonito, are obvious exceptions.) Small fish may be scaled with the fingertips or the back edge of a small knife. Large fish such as salmon or seabass are easily scaled with a *fish scaler* shown on page 18. With either tool, scrape from the tail toward the head to remove all the scales, and rinse the skin to remove any clinging scales. For easy clean-up, work on top of several thicknesses of brown paper or newspaper to catch the scales. After scaling, the fish may be dressed, pan-dressed or boned, as desired.

Dressing a Fish

1 Make a shallow cut, blade pointing outward, from the vent to the chin, being careful not to pierce the entrails.

2 With two short cuts, free the bottom of the gills from the chin and from the belly flesh.

3 Pull the operculum open to expose the gills. Cut the top of the gills free from the head. The gills should now be attached only to the entrails.

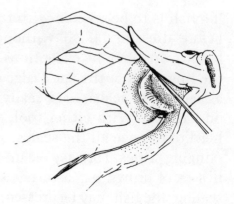

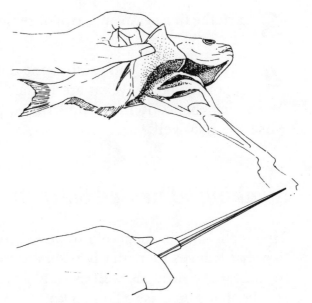

4 Pin the gills to the board with the tip of the knife. Draw the fish away; the entrails should pull away from the body along with the gills. Remove the kidneys (the strip of reddish tissue near the backbone) and any other material left in the cavity, and rinse well.

Pan-Dressing a Small Flatfish

This technique, illustrated here on a sand dab, works equally well for horizontally compressed fish such as butterfish, surf-perch and freshwater "panfish" such as bluegill. Work with a large French knife or Chinese cleaver, starting with the point of the knife on the board as if slicing vegetables.

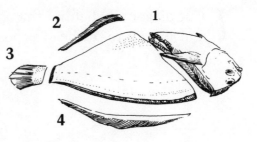

1 Start with the fish oriented as shown. Make one decisive cut from just behind the head to behind the vent, removing the head, gills and entrails in one piece. (Feel for the point where filet stops and the belly cavity begins, and cut just behind this point.)

2 Turn the fish 90° clockwise. Remove the anal fin together with the short bones which support it and the attached strips of soft flesh. Save these for the stock pot.

3 Turn the fish again and trim or remove the tail fin.

4 Turn once more and remove the dorsal fin, again with the supporting bones. What are left are the two filets attached to the backbone. Remove any traces of kidney and roe and rinse the fish well.

Steaking a Dressed Salmon

This technique is adaptable to any similarly sized and shaped fish. It produces four filet portions, two from the tail and two from near the head, as well as steaks from the central section. For the first steps, use a French knife or Chinese cleaver for best results.

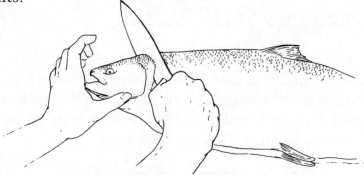

1 Cut diagonally behind the operculum, as close to the bone and as far into the head as possible.

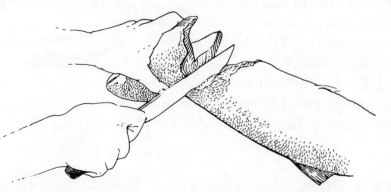

2 Turn the fish over and repeat. Sever the backbone to remove the head.

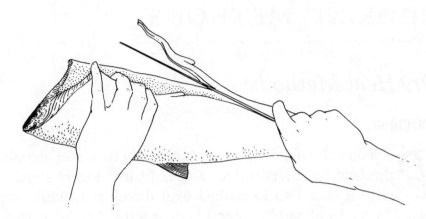

3 Trim the flap of belly flesh by about an inch, if desired. (This is the fattest and least desirable part of the meat.)

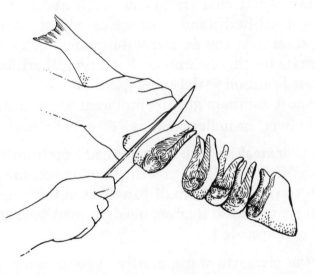

4 Using a steaking knife (see page 18) or a French knife make the first cut perpendicular to the backbone about 4 inches from the head end. Slice the fish into steaks, ¾–1½ inches thick, to approximately the point of the anal fin. If the backbone is particularly large you can force the knife through it by hitting the blade with a rubber mallet (see page 18). Filet the head and tail portions or reserve them for cooking whole.

COOKING METHODS

Dry Heat Methods

GRILLING

*P*ROBABLY the oldest method of cooking fish, and arguably the best, is directly over a fire. In its modern version, grilling, the fish is cooked over direct heat while supported by a grill of parallel metal bars or wire. The heat source may be charcoal or wood, a gas flame or an electric heating element. The fish is cooked both by direct heat and by heat transmitted through the grill bars, which typically leave a pattern of dark searing marks on the cooked surface.

Most grilled seafood benefits from a preliminary oil-based marinade. Additional flavor can be introduced by throwing fresh or dried herbs and herb stems on the coals as the fish cooks; rosemary, thyme and wild fennel stalks are especially appropriate for this treatment. For a typical grilling procedure, see Grilled Salmon with Fennel (page 187).

The most common grilling problems are fish sticking to the grill and over- or under-cooking. To avoid these:

Oil filets or steaks which have not had a preliminary marinade, draining off excess oil to prevent flare-ups on the grill. (An exception to this rule is small pan-dressed flatfish, which seem more likely to stick if they are oiled; they are best grilled without any oil or marinade.)

Allow the pieces to warm briefly to room temperature before cooking. This allows the heat to penetrate to the center more quickly without overcooking the outside. (This advice applies to other cooking methods as well.)

Preheat the grill thoroughly. Fish will nearly always stick to a cold grill.

Work with a hot fire. Mexican mesquite charcoal or hardwood produces a hotter fire than briquets and imparts a nicer aroma.

Generally speaking, if you can hold your hand a few inches above the grill for any length of time, the fire is not hot enough. Set electric or other indoor grills to maximum heat.

Maintain the grill surface carefully during and after use. Clean the grill with a wire brush between rounds of grilling, and oil after cleaning as you would a cast-iron skillet.

Position fish carefully to minimize contact with the grill. Whether cooking whole fish or filets, place them perpendicular to the grill bars rather than parallel. Start filets skin side up for the best presentation.

Try to turn fish only once, and present the fish with the first-cooked side (bone side) up. Remember that a piece may cook more or less than halfway on the first side, and adjust the time for the second side accordingly. Avoid excessive handling of the fish. The more times a piece is moved, the more chances it has to stick. If the piece will not lift easily with tongs or the long edge of an offset spatula, let it sit another half minute or so before you try again.

BROILING

One step removed from grilling is broiling, which exposes the fish to high direct overhead heat. Almost any kind of fish filet or steak as well as small whole fish may be broiled. Lean fish, however, are prone to drying out quickly when broiled; they should be basted with an oil-based marinade or a compound butter to prevent this. Thin filets and steaks will cook through from one side, but larger pieces will generally require turning. For a detailed broiling procedure, see Broiled Sablefish with Anchovy Butter (page 183).

FRYING

Perhaps the most popular method of fish cookery in the world is frying (or "deep frying" as it is frequently and redundantly called). Many dishes which are commonly described as "fried" are actually sautéed, stir-fried or pan-fried (see pages 32–33 for a description of these techniques).

32   Fried foods are those which are immersed in hot fat, either vegetable or animal, and cooked without contact with the cooking vessel. Most frying involves a batter or a dry coating of flour, cornmeal or the like which seals in the flavors and juices and prevents absorption of excess fat. Properly fried foods are crisp on the outside and steaming hot inside; little or none of the cooking oil should remain on or in the food. Improperly fried foods, however, may absorb large quantities of fat and be difficult to digest, or be well-browned on the outside but only partially cooked inside.

Unless otherwise specified, all recipes for fried seafood in this book require a mild-flavored vegetable oil such as peanut or safflower. The ideal temperature for most frying is between 350° and 375°. For examples of this technique, see Sweet and Sour Fish (page 79).

Frying with consistently good results is a skill which takes practice and careful attention. The following are some common problems and ways in which to avoid them:

Greasy or soggy coating is caused by cooking at too low a temperature. Start with the oil around 375° (a fat thermometer is helpful). Avoid adding too many pieces at once; if the oil does not return to at least 325–350° quickly after the fish is added, you are frying too much at a time.

Dark coating or burnt flavor is caused by either too high a temperature or oil which has been overheated or overused. Skim any bits of batter from the oil before they burn, and discard oil which has darkened noticeably or has a burnt aroma.

Batter falling off in frying or serving is caused by applying batter to wet pieces or by excessive handling in the battering process. Dry the fish pieces before battering, and try to keep one hand dry when making the batter.

SAUTÉING

Sautéing is cooking food in a shallow pan with a small amount of fat over moderate to high heat. The heat is transmitted to the food both by the pan and by the cooking fat. Generally, pieces of food are either turned or otherwise moved during the cooking process to evenly heat all surfaces. Sauces for sautéed fish are frequently made in the pan after the fish has been cooked and removed, and may involve all or part of the cooking fat. For an example of this technique, see Sautéed Halibut with Cream and Herbs (page 128).

PAN-FRYING AND STIR-FRYING

"Pan-frying" and Oriental "stir-frying" are essentially variations on sautéing techniques. In pan-frying, relatively large pieces are cooked in a generous amount of fat and turned once. In stir-frying, the ingredients are generally cut more finely and cooked in almost constant motion. As with sautéing, recipes for either pan-frying or stir-frying frequently involve a sauce made with some of the cooking fat. For an example of these techniques, see Kung Pao Shrimp (page 208).

Stir-frying has its own set of rules. For the best results, pay strict attention to the timing and keep the following in mind:

Cut foods into uniform pieces for uniform cooking time.

Add ingredients to the wok or pan according to their relative cooking times. Be careful with chopped garlic, ginger and the like which are typically added early to flavor the oil, but which burn easily.

Keep the food pieces in constant motion to cook all surfaces evenly.

Use sufficient oil to cook all the ingredients, at least at the early stages. Excess oil may be removed before adding sauce ingredients.

BAKING

Baking is cooking wrapped or unwrapped foods in an oven, with heat ranging from moderate to high. Because of the time required to cook fish by baking, it must be enclosed somehow to prevent its drying out. This may be achieved by baking in a covered dish, entirely wrapping the fish in a package of paper or foil, or battering the fish as for frying. The first two methods are ideal for baking fish with aromatic vegetables or herbs; the

34   steam released by the cooking fish combines with the other flavors to produce a nice sauce. For an example of this technique, see Baked Rockfish Veracruz Style (page 173). Baking in a batter, or in puff pastry or filo dough, provides an edible coating which still seals in most of the moisture and flavor. For an example of this technique, see Angler Baked in Filo (page 58).

Moist Heat Methods

BRAISING

Braising is actually a hybrid of dry and moist cooking methods. The food is first cooked quickly in oil to seal the outside flesh, then liquid is added for the remaining cooking time. Braising fish permits more exchange of flavors between the fish and sauce than does a simple sauté with sauce, but less than stewing. Braising is ideal for combining ingredients with assertive flavors, such as olives, anchovies, garlic, ginger and curry.

For a detailed braising procedure, see Braised Mackerel with Tomatoes, Rosemary and Garlic (page 145).

STEWING

Stews are combinations of foods cooked and served in liquids without the initial dry-cooking step of braising. Stewing is generally a longer and slower process than braising, and it produces a more complete exchange of flavors. Examples of stewing are California "Bouillabaisse" (page 179) and Laotian Catfish Soup (page 85).

STEAMING

Steaming is cooking in an enclosed vessel over boiling water, wine or an aromatic liquid, which is then discarded. Of all moist heat methods of cooking fish, steaming produces the best-textured flesh, although with only a slight interchange of flavors. Whole fish, steaks or filets may be steamed.

A variety of equipment may be used for steaming fish (see page 64). We recommend steaming on a plate in a wok as the most practical way to retain the liquids released from the

fish in cooking. These are often the base of a sauce, along with
soy sauce, fish sauce or vegetables. For a typical steaming procedure, see page 64.

"STEAMING" SHELLFISH

"Steaming" also describes a slightly different technique for
cooking clams or mussels in the shell. The shellfish are placed
in a saucepan with a small amount of liquid (and usually garlic
and herbs), covered and brought to a boil. The shellfish cook in
both the boiling liquid and the trapped steam, opening their
shells when they die. The liquid released from the shells, together with the remaining cooking liquid, is then served with
the shellfish or incorporated into a sauce.

POACHING

Poaching is cooking by immersion in simmering (*not* boiling)
flavored liquid. Properly done, poaching produces some of the
most delicate seafood dishes. The liquid may be Court-Bouillon
(page 251), Fumet (page 252) or simply water flavored with
wine and a few herbs.

Poaching techniques vary, except for the common rule that
the liquid must never reach the boiling point. Small filets and
thin steaks may be directly immersed in simmering liquid to
cook in just a few minutes. Filets with a stuffing are more easily
handled by placing them in the poaching pan and pouring the
separately heated liquid over them. Larger pieces or whole fish
are typically started in cold or lukewarm liquid which is then
heated to a simmer. Large fish, such as salmon, may be wrapped
in cheesecloth before cooking for ease of handling the cooked
fish. For larger filets, steaks or whole fish, allow about 8 minutes per inch of thickness after the liquid begins to steam.

After poaching fish in *court-bouillon*, you will be left with a
sort of weak *fumet*. Some poached fish preparations use a reduction of this liquid in the accompanying sauce. Otherwise,
it may be strained and reserved for another use. Poached fish is
frequently served cold with a mayonnaise (pages 257–59) or
another cold sauce. For poaching procedures, see Poached Salmon
(page 186) and Filet of Sole Stuffed with Shrimp (page 220).

BOILING

There are two instances where we recommend boiling seafood: cooking live shellfish, especially crab and crayfish, and blanching squid in rapidly boiling salted water for use in salads and Squid Stuffing for Pasta (page 229).

SPECIAL INGREDIENTS

*A*N *important feature of "California cuisine" is the availability of a number of special ingredients—herbs, spices, condiments and exotic vegetables often associated with a given ethnic cuisine. What follows is a selected list of the special ingredients used in our recipes, including their typical sources and recipes for possible substitutions, if any.*

Achiote or **Annato seed:** The seed of a tree found in tropical America. The seeds are ground, usually with other spices, to produce a paste. Achiote is sold in Latin American groceries and in many supermarkets.

Anchovies: Canned anchovies vary widely in quality and saltiness. Most are packed in oil, but some well-stocked delicatessens carry salt-packed whole anchovies, which are more delicate in flavor. After a can of these is opened, however, they should then be stored in oil, preferably in good olive oil. When anchovies are used in slow-cooking dishes, their saltiness will permeate the dish, making additional salt unnecessary. For most other uses, however, rinse the filets of excess salt and oil before adding to the dish.

Basil: Use basil with garlic in hot butters or herb mayonnaise, or in sauces involving tomato. The dried herb is a poor substitute.

Bay: Use imported bay leaves for the most delicate flavor. The California bay laurel, a common tree in many parts of the state, yields a pungent, strong-flavored leaf which should be used sparingly.

Butter: We recommend unsalted ("sweet") butter in all recipes. If this is unavailable, remember to decrease the salt.

Celery: Celery is generally thought of as a vegetable, but the leaves from the heart are useful in a *bouquet garni*. Use with caution in making *fumet* or *court-bouillon*, as its flavor can easily dominate.

Chervil: Chervil is a delightful but relatively little-known herb which resembles a mild, sweet parsley with overtones of anise. It is only useful fresh; dried, it has almost no flavor or aroma. Use in compound butters, herb mayonnaise, or other simple sauces.

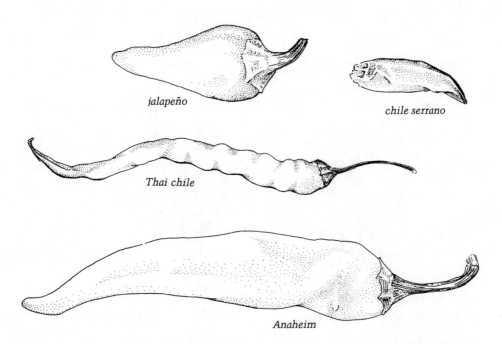

jalapeño

chile serrano

Thai chile

Anaheim

Chiles: Most of the chile varieties listed below are also available in ripened and dried form. Fresh chile peppers range widely in size and flavor, from the 6- to 8-inch mild Anaheim to the 2-inch very hot *chile serrano*. These two varieties are the most widely available. You may also find others, including the large, dark green, richly flavored *chile poblano*, the medium to hot

38 green Fresno and yellow wax varieties, and the long slender red type sold mainly in Philippine and other Asian markets. Several recipes in this book call for whole small dried chiles; the varieties labeled *chile japonés* or *serrano seco* in Latin American markets or simply "whole red pepper" in Asian markets are appropriate. Note that "chile powder" is simply ground dried chiles while "chili powder" is a blend of chile powder and other spices such as garlic and oregano.

Chives: Use chives for a mild onion flavor in cold or hot sauces. Like all onions, they will grow stronger after cutting; avoid keeping chive sauces overnight.

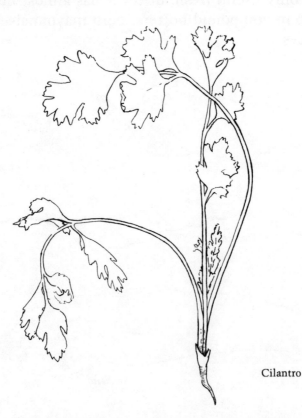

Cilantro

Cilantro: Cilantro or coriander (also known as Chinese parsley) is a pungent herb grown in most of the tropical and semi-tropical regions of the world. The root is stronger than the leaves and should not be used unless the recipe specifically calls for it.

Coconut milk: An extract made from the flesh of the coconut (not the juice inside the shell), coconut milk is available canned or you can make your own. It is easiest to prepare with dry shredded coconut although grated fresh coconut makes a slightly richer milk. Combine equal parts coconut and boiling water in a blender or food processor (be careful when starting the machine so as not to scald yourself). Blend for 1 minute. Strain through a fine sieve or cheesecloth. The yield is about three-quarters of the amount of water added. You can use the same coconut twice; the second batch is often referred to as thin coconut milk.

Cooking oils: Unless a specific oil such as olive or sesame is called for, "oil" in these recipes means a vegetable oil of relatively neutral flavor. We prefer peanut, but safflower and sunflower are perfectly acceptable. Frying oil may be filtered and reserved for additional frying until it darkens noticeably or develops a cooked aroma.

Crème Fraîche: The French term for a type of thick, ripened cream with excellent cooking qualities. Its flavor is less sour than commercial sour cream with a slight nuttiness, and it is unmatched for cream-reduction sauces.

> Yield: 1 cup
> ½ pint whipping cream
> 2 tablespoons cultured buttermilk
>
> Combine the cream and buttermilk in a non-aluminum saucepan, heat to 85–90° (higher heat will inhibit the culture) and transfer to a warmed glass, earthenware or stainless bowl. Cover, place in a warm spot and allow to ripen at least 6 hours or overnight. The cream should have a texture between that of fresh cream and yogurt.

Dill: Use dill in simple hot or cold butters, as its flavor will be lost in more complicated sauces. Especially well-suited to trout and salmon.

Fennel: Fennel is a name loosely given to several related plants. Commercial bulb fennel, which is used as a vegetable, is also frequently labeled "sweet anise." Its foliage, as well as that of

40   the wild variety, can be used as an herb in butters and marinades. The wild variety, common in coastal California, has fibrous, inedible stems which are an excellent addition to a charcoal fire, adding their fragrant smoke to that of the charcoal. Both types provide edible seeds in the fall.

Fish Sauce: Fish sauce is a clear, dark extract made from fermented salted anchovies. It is used as we would use salt in much of Southeast Asia, including Thailand, Laos, Vietnam, Cambodia and the Philippines. Fish sauce is sold at most Asian groceries and in some supermarkets. Anchovy paste is not a good substitute.

Five Spice Powder: Five spice powder is a fragrant Chinese mixture composed of black pepper, fennel seed, cinnamon, cloves and star anise. It is sold bottled or packaged in Asian groceries and in many supermarkets.

Garam Masala: *Garam masala* is an Indian spice mixture used much the same way we employ salt and pepper. It is added just before the food is served or during the last couple of minutes of cooking. Recipes for *garam masala* vary, but they usually contain cardamom, cloves, cinnamon, coriander, cumin and black pepper. *Garam masala* is sold in Indian groceries, or you can make your own using freshly ground spices in these proportions (by volume): 1 part each cumin, coriander and cinnamon; 2 parts black peppercorns; ½ part cloves; 1½ parts cardamom.

Herbs: A wide range of herbs are useful in seafood cookery. The milder herbs, such as parsley, chervil and chives, are the most useful and versatile; at least one of these appears in almost every Western recipe in this book. The milder herbs provide a background of flavor without upstaging the other ingredients. Others with more pronounced flavors are more limited in use, and are often sufficient in themselves to give a whole new dimension to a dish. Use fresh herbs whenever possible. Many are easily grown outdoors (all year in mild climates) or indoors on a windowsill. As a general rule, use a quarter to half as much dried herbs as fresh. Even with dried herbs, relative freshness is important, and they lose their potency over time. Herbs in half-empty, year-old jars are unlikely to have much flavor.

Laos Root: Laos root is an important ingredient in the cooking of Southeast Asia, particularly in Thailand and Laos. It has a strong, slightly medicinal taste. Ginger is *not* a particularly good substitute. Laos root is sold dried and in powder form (often under the name of *galangal*) in Asian groceries. To use dried Laos root, soak it in water for at least 3 hours. The powdered root has less flavor and is a second choice.

Lemongrass

Lemongrass: Lemongrass is a pungent herb of the tropics whose taste is somewhat like lemon blossoms. It is a major flavoring in much of Southeast Asia. Lemongrass is available fresh in a growing number of produce markets and in some Asian groceries. Dried lemongrass is available in health food stores and some supermarkets. The fresh is much preferable. Dried lemongrass should be soaked in water for at least 30 minutes. Lemon peel and fresh ginger together form a passable substitute.

Marjoram, Oregano: Closely related and similar in use, oregano and marjoram are primarily for dishes involving tomato, olive oil and garlic. Both are a good addition to olive oil marinades for grilled fish, and the stems and additional sprigs can be thrown on the fire for fragrant smoke.

Mirin: A sweet rice wine produced in Japan and recently in the United States, it contains 10–12% alcohol. In recipes calling for dry sherry or dry rice wine *and* sugar, you can substitute *mirin* and eliminate most of the sugar. *Mirin* is sold in Asian groceries and in some liquor stores and supermarkets.

Olive Oil: Olive oil is used in many Mediterranean-based dishes in this book. As its purpose is to add a distinctive flavor to the dish, choose an oil with some flavor, something which is lacking in many widely available, overly refined oils. Extremely fine oils labeled Virgin or Extra Virgin are now available in many markets at prices ranging from expensive to astronomical; however, a small amount of one of these mixed with a commercial brand produces a very nicely flavored oil. With some experimenting, you should be able to arrive at a delicious and reasonably priced "house blend."

Parsley: Use flat-leaved Italian parsley if a stonger flavor is desired.

Rice Wine Vinegar: Rice wine vinegar is a mild white vinegar distilled from rice wine. It is often used in Japanese cooking and can usually be substituted for distilled white vinegar in other recipes. It is sold in Asian groceries and in many supermarkets.

Rosemary: Rosemary will dominate most dishes; use with care, alone or with other assertive flavors. This herb is best for rich, flavorful fish such as mackerel, and unsurpassed as an addition to a charcoal fire.

Saké: Saké is a Japanese rice wine which contains about 16% alcohol. It is slightly sweeter than a dry European or American white wine. It can be substituted for Chinese rice wine (*Shao Hsing*) without altering the recipe. Saké is sold at Asian groceries, supermarkets and many liquor stores.

Salted Black Beans: Salted black beans are fermented and dried in Canton, the only part of China where they are used. They are the key ingredient in black bean sauce. Salted black beans are sold packaged in plastic bags in Asian groceries and in some supermarkets.

Sesame Seeds: Both white and black sesame seeds are available in this country. White sesame seeds are used as a coating for Chinese fish dishes. Sesame seeds are sold in bulk in health food stores and packaged in Asian groceries and in some supermarkets.

Sesame Oil: Sesame oil is a very powerful flavoring agent made from toasted sesame seeds and not to be confused with the cold-pressed sesame oil available in health food stores. It is not a cooking oil, but is added in small quantities just before serving, releasing its perfume as it warms with the food.

Shao Hsing Wine: *Shao Hsing* wine is a rice wine nearly as dry as western white wines. It can be used in place of saké. It is sold in Asian groceries and in some liquor stores.

Shrimp Paste: Shrimp paste is a strong, salty extract made from dried shrimp. Each country has its own version, varying greatly in saltiness and strength. In Chinese recipes try to use Chinese shrimp paste, etc. Shrimp paste is sold in Asian groceries and in some supermarkets.

Sichuan Bean Paste: Sichuan bean paste is a pungent, spicy fermented mixture usually sold under the name "chili paste with garlic" in Asian groceries. It will keep almost indefinitely if stored in the refrigerator. There is no substitute.

Soy Sauce: Soy sauce is produced in three principal grades: (1) light—labeled "light," (2) medium—which has no particular labeling and includes most soy sauce sold in this country, and (3) dark—often labeled "black." These three grades differ mostly in coloring rather than in taste. Unless otherwise noted, use medium soy sauce for the recipes in this book.

Tamarind: Tamarind is produced from the pulp of the pod of a tropical plant. Its tart flavor appears in many Southeast Asian, Indian and Latin American dishes. Tamarind is sold fresh in some specialty shops and produce markets. It is also available as a paste or extract which is added to water. Lemon juice is not a particularly good substitute since the sour taste of tamarind is distinctive. Tamarind extract keeps in the refrigerator for months.

Tarragon: Tarragon is fairly assertive, and not very compatible with other herbs. It is the essential ingredient in Béarnaise Sauce (page 257). If unavailable fresh, use whole leaves bottled in vinegar.

Thai Basil: Thai basil is a highly aromatic herb which can be transplanted if you can find somebody with plants already growing. Its flavor is something of a cross between mint and Italian basil. Use both together as a substitute for Thai basil.

Tomatoes: Tomatoes are a common ingredient in seafood dishes

44 from the Mediterranean and the Americas. While we generally recommend using fresh produce wherever possible, the only tomatoes available for much of the year are watery, mushy and tasteless due to early harvest or mass growing techniques. When properly ripened, flavorful tomatoes are available, by all means use them. However, during the many months when fresh tomatoes are only available by the miracles of modern science, we find good canned tomatoes superior in flavor and more attractive in price. Italian tomato varieties seem to preserve the best. Better still, buy them in quantity during the peak of the season and can them yourself.

To peel and seed tomatoes: Have ready a large bowl of ice water. Cut the cores from the tomatoes and slash the skin in a cross pattern with the tip of a knife. Plunge the tomatoes into rapidly boiling water, remove them as soon as the skin begins to peel back from the cuts, and transfer them to the ice water to cool. The skins should peel away easily, leaving the barely cooked flesh intact. Slice the tomatoes in half crosswise to expose all the seeds. Gently squeeze the seeds and excess juice from the tomato halves, straining and reserving the juice if it is to be used in the recipe.

Tomatillos: *Tomatillos*, despite the name, are not related to the tomato but are a type of berry. They can sometimes be found fresh in Latin American markets, and have a papery husk covering the smooth green skin. They are widely available canned, with the confusing label "Mexican green tomatoes." There is no substitute.

Thyme: Thyme is a most useful herb, and a standard ingredient in a *bouquet garni*. There are many varieties, some with lemon or other flavors. Its agreeable flavor blends well with other herbs.

Wasabi: *Wasabi* is green horseradish powder made in Japan. It is used with soy sauce as a dip for *sushi* and incorporated into other raw fish dishes. It is sold in small tins in Asian groceries and in many supermarkets.

Watercress: Use watercress sparingly in compound butters for its peppery, slightly bitter flavor.

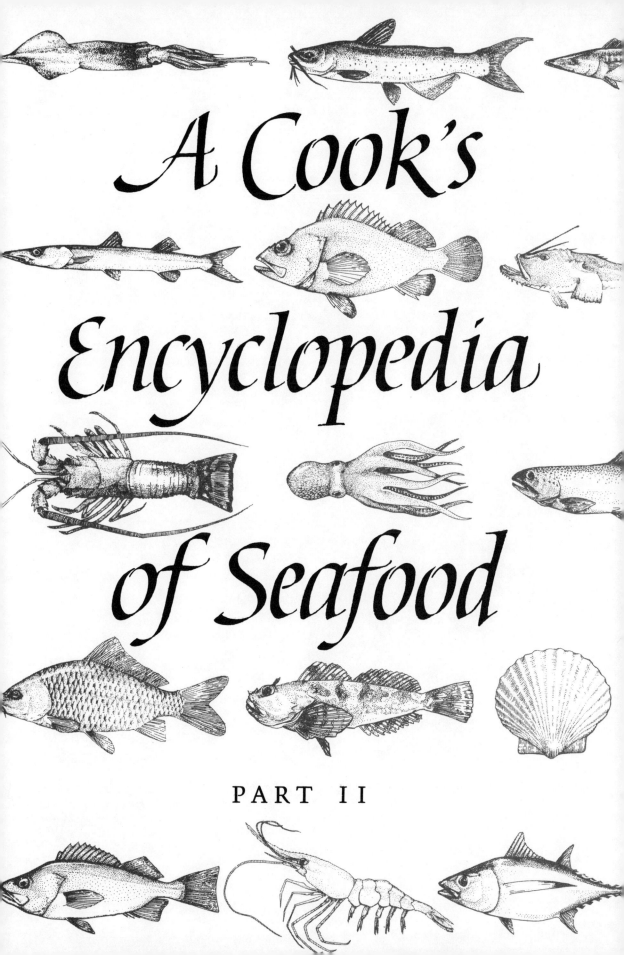

A Cook's
Encyclopedia
of Seafood

PART II

KEY TO
ENCYCLOPEDIC ENTRIES

*T*HE *following encyclopedic entries are concise profiles of fish typically available in the market or commonly caught by sportsmen in California. Exceptions to the listed seasons, sizes and ranges will, of course, occur. We have also listed many species available fresh in California from other regions of the country. (Where categories are not relevant to a particular species, they are left out.).*

Name: *Common and Latin names follow Miller and Lea (1972). (See Bibliography, page 283)*

Other Names: *These are primarily other names by which the fish may be marketed; some are common fishermen's names.*

Description: *Primarily color. A description such as "blue-green fading to silver" refers to the typical pattern of shading, dorsal to ventral sides.*

Size: *Overall size range as well as normal market size are given.*

Range: *Listed south to north. Some species may occur outside the ranges given, but these represent the areas where they are typically caught.*

Season: *Again, these are typical seasons. Availability of many species depends upon water temperature and food supply, which can vary considerably from one year to the next. Commercial seasons may also be regulated by government agencies, opening and closing on short notice due to population monitoring, parasite incidence or other considerations.*

Fat Content: *Lean fish are those which carry little or no fat in the muscle tissues, storing it instead in the liver or other organs. Others contain more or less fat in the meat, ranging from about 6% in herring to over 20% in eel.*

48 **Yield:** *Unless otherwise noted, yield figures are given as a percentage of the weight of a round fish, based upon the forms recommended for cooking—steaks and filets of salmon, pan-dressed rex sole, edible portion of squid, etc.*

Available Forms: *Forms are described on page 13. When a species is available in several forms, we have listed the more common or preferred form first.*

Similar Species: *These are either related to the listed species or otherwise similar; they may or may not be suitable alternatives, as noted in each entry.*

Alternatives: *Where other species are similar enough in cooking characteristics that they may be used in all recipes for the main species, they are listed in the encyclopedic entry. See the individual recipes for other specific alternatives.*

(A), (G) and (P) are used as a quick reference guide to the geographic range of suggested alternatives—Atlantic, Gulf of Mexico and Pacific. Species exclusive to the Pacific have no special designation.

How to Locate Recipes

There are two places in this book to find recipes for a given species: first, following the species' entry in the Encyclopedia; second, in the Index where additional recipes for which a species is an *alternative* are cited under the common name.

Notes on Recipes

Please don't overcook fish! Personal tastes vary, but for our purposes fish is done when the center of the thickest part of the fish is just about to lose its translucency. Remember that a piece of fish will continue cooking for a few minutes after removal from the heat.

Cooking times are approximate. There are so many variables—size of fish, oven and grill temperatures, heat conductivity of pans and so on—that these times should be taken as general guidelines. Familiarity with your own cooking equipment is essential for the best results.

Several recipes mention the "skewer test." A thin metal or bamboo skewer is a perfect instrument for gently probing the flesh of a cooking piece of fish. Try it on a piece of raw fish, then again during the cooking process, and finally with a cooked piece to get the feel of the various stages. This technique can also be used as a test for fish baking in foil or in other situations where testing with the eye or fingertip is impractical.

Most of these recipes do not specify quantities of salt, suggesting instead "salt to taste." Increasing awareness of the health risks of too much sodium has caused us to adjust our thinking on proper levels of salt. Our own tastes have been shifting somewhat in recent years to less reliance on salt for flavoring the foods we eat. Bear in mind also that many of the ingredients used throughout this book (anchovies, olives, capers, soy sauce, fish sauce and so on) contain substantial salt and are sufficient to flavor the dishes in which they appear.

Most of the recipes allow 4–6 ounces of fish per serving as main courses. They may, of course, be adjusted up or down according to personal preferences. Many of the Asian recipes also give a

50 yield in terms of side-dish servings, where the dish is one of several courses in a meal.

All of the recipes have been written for 4 servings unless this number is inappropriate. Large-scale productions such as Crab Gumbo (page 113) are most likely to be served at a large gathering rather than at a small family dinner. The variety of fish required for our Bouillabaisse (page 179) makes it difficult to prepare on a small scale. On the other hand, where the recipe is difficult to increase beyond 2 servings, such as Warm Cabbage Salad with Angler (page 60), the recipe is given for the smaller number.

Alternative species have been suggested whenever appropriate. They have been chosen for their basic similarity in flavor, texture or cooking characteristics. However, we are not suggesting that you will get identical results, only that you need not rule out a recipe just because a particular fish is unavailable.

We have included recommendations for side dishes, garnishes or vegetable accompaniments in some cases but we have not tried to present whole menus, which we leave to the reader. Similarly, we have not given specific suggestions for wines or other beverages other than the general guidelines in the section Wine and Seafood (pages 276–77).

CALIFORNIA SEAFOOD A–Z

ABALONE
(Haliotis spp.*)*

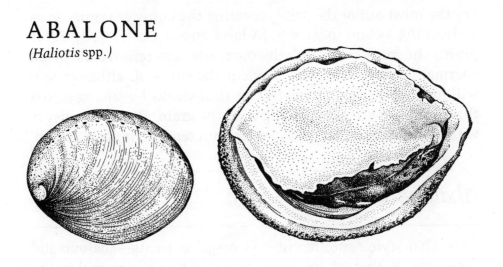

Description: *Univalve. Outside of shell usually encrusted with barnacles, inside of shell iridescent shades of pink, blue and green.*	**Season:** *Highly regulated. Sporadically available May– March.*
	Fat Content: *Low.*
Size: *5¾–8 inches legal minimum, depending on species.*	**Yield:** *If overall live weight is over 1 pound, yield is 50% meat with an additional 25% usable trim.*
Range: *Highest concentrations of edible species found along the coasts of Japan, Australia and California.*	**Available Forms:** *Live, tenderized steaks.*

Black, red and green abalone are the most commonly available live varieties. Abalone is rapidly disappearing due to overfishing and natural predation. However, it is being aquacultured and may make something of a comeback. California abalone cannot be shipped out of the state in any form; abalone available elsewhere comes from Mexico and Japan.

Abalone is very tough and must be pounded before cooking. Pounded steaks are usually floured or dipped in egg and sautéed over very high heat for 20–30 seconds per side. Longer cooking will toughen the meat. Like whelk, abalone makes excellent Ceviche (page 70).

To Clean Abalone

Pry the meat out of the shell, severing the connector muscle as if shucking a clam (page 89). (A large spoon works well.) After prying the meat out, scrub the outer edges to remove the black coating. (If you prefer, you may cut the edges off although you will lose a good deal of meat.) Cut thin steaks by slicing across the muscle, or strips by slicing with the grain. Pound the pieces with a mallet or the side of a cleaver until tender but not shredded.

Abalone in Oyster Sauce

This Thai-style sauté features two spring treats—abalone and asparagus. Both cook at about the same rate which makes the dish easy to prepare.

Alternatives: *Whelk (A,P), geoduck*

Serves 4-6 as a side dish

2 tablespoons oil

1-2 tablespoons chopped garlic

2 teaspoons chopped ginger

2 tablespoons Chinese oyster sauce

2 teaspoons fish sauce (page 40)

2 tablespoons water

½ pound abalone meat, pounded and cut into narrow strips 1½ inches long

1 pound asparagus, cut into 2-inch lengths

¼ cup loosely packed cilantro

1 teaspoon cornstarch dissolved in 1 tablespoon water

Sauté the garlic and ginger in oil in a wok or heavy skillet until nearly cooked. Add the oyster sauce, fish sauce and water. Bring to a boil. Add the abalone and asparagus. Cook over high heat for about 3 minutes or until the asparagus is tender. One minute before the dish is done, add the cilantro and stir the ingredients thoroughly. Pour in the cornstarch mixture. When the sauce thickens, remove the skillet from the heat. Serve over rice.

ANCHOVY

(Engraulis mordax)

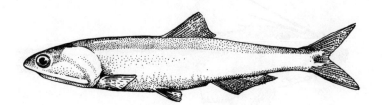

Description: *Blue-green fading to silver.*	**Fat Content:** *High.*
Size: *4–5 inches.*	**Yield:** *50% filet.*
Range: *Pacific coast.*	**Available Forms:** *Round.*
Season: *Fall–Winter.*	

The Pacific anchovy catch is now only a fraction of its peak of earlier years due to a combination of overfishing and environmental influences. Most of today's catch is preserved for commercial use as a favorite bait for salmon fishing.

Fresh anchovies are, however, occasionally available. Their soft flesh has a moderate-to-pronounced flavor similar to herring and sardines, to which they are related. The extreme saltiness associated with preserved anchovies is part of the canning process, not an inherent characteristic of the fish.

Pan-dressed anchovies may be grilled or floured and fried. (To pan-dress anchovies or similar small fish, simply grasp the head and twist, drawing the entrails away with the head.) Larger anchovies are suitable for most herring recipes (pages 132–35).

ANGLER

(Lophius americanus)

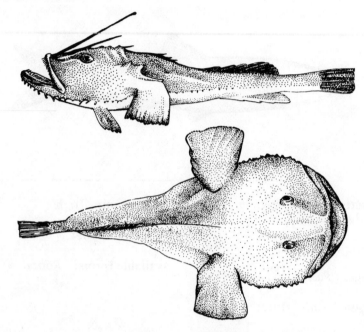

Other Names: *Goosefish, monkfish, lotte.*	**Season:** *Year-round, especially fall-winter.*
Description: *Loose, scaleless skin. Variegated brown to black fading to light grey.*	**Fat Content:** *Low.*
	Yield: *50–60% filet from tail.*
Size: *2–50 pounds (larger fish more desirable).*	**Available Forms:** *Whole or boneless tail.*
Range: *New England coast. Also Mediterranean and eastern Atlantic.*	

This exceedingly ugly but delicious fish is well-known around the Mediterranean and along our Atlantic coast, and is becoming more popular and available fresh in the west. Its name comes from its unique method of attracting prey by "angling" with a small appendage on top of its head as "bait." Only the tail is generally marketed, the huge head being discarded at sea.

Angler flesh is dense and firm with a mild, sweet flavor which has been compared to lobster. (In fact, shellfish make up an important part of its diet.) Angler is suitable for almost any cooking method, and is nearly indispensible in *bouillabaisse*. Its large single bone makes a particularly rich and gelatinous stock.

To Filet an Angler

1 Remove the loose outer skin from the tail.
Trim the dorsal fin if desired. (Note: For grilled butterfly filets, also remove all of the thin membrane under the skin, or it will shrink in cooking and distort the filet.)

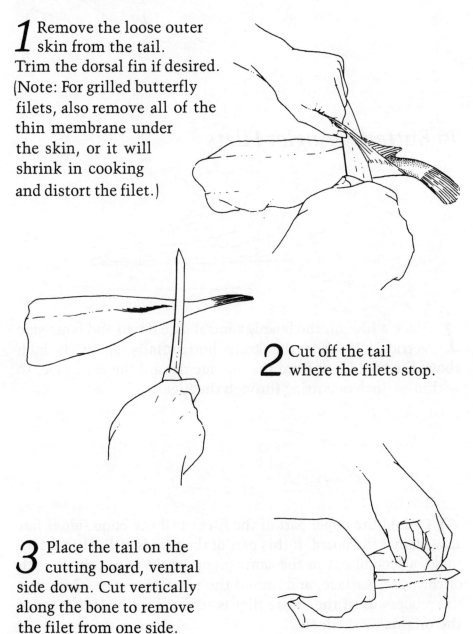

2 Cut off the tail where the filets stop.

3 Place the tail on the cutting board, ventral side down. Cut vertically along the bone to remove the filet from one side.

4 Repeat on the other side of the bone. Reserve all the bones, skin and trimmings for the stock pot.

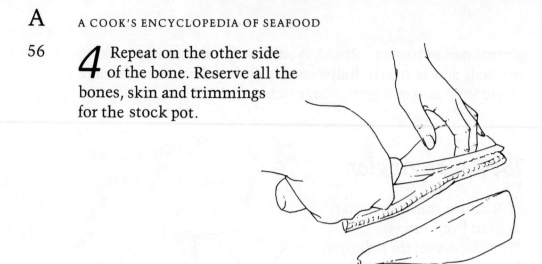

To Butterfly Angler Filets

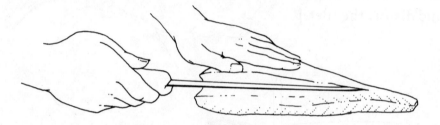

1 Place a filet on the board, ventral side down and bone side vertical. Holding the knife horizontally about ⅜ inch above the board, cut from the outside toward the bone side, to within ¼ inch of cutting through the filet.

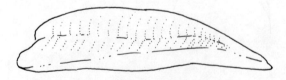

2 Unfold the upper part of the filet until the bone side is flat against the board. If this part of the filet is still quite thick, make a second cut in the same plane, again to within ¼ inch of the outer surface, and unfold the remaining part. Continue the process until the entire filet is reduced to the thickness of the original ¾-inch cut.

Grilled Angler Filet

Because of its dense flesh, angler must be cut into thin pieces to grill easily. The best technique is the continuous butterfly cut described on the previous page. An alternative method is to slice the filet crosswise into ⅜–½-inch pieces and grill them on skewers.

Serves 4

4 6-ounce filets	*Fresh herbs*
Olive oil	*Salt and pepper to taste*

Marinate the cut filets in olive oil and fresh herbs. Grill until done by the skewer test. Serve with Beurre Blanc (page 253) or another delicately flavored sauce.

Baked Angler with Sicilian-Style Stuffing

Serves 4

A 1½-pound piece of angler

Stuffing

¼ cup bread crumbs	*3 cloves chopped garlic*
¼ cup raisins	*1 tablespoon olive oil*
2 tablespoons chopped parsley	*1 tablespoon lemon juice*
2 tablespoons chopped capers	*Tomato slices for garnish*
2 tablespoons pine nuts	

Preheat the oven to 350°.

Cut the angler butterfly style.

Combine the stuffing ingredients. Spread the stuffing across the fish. Roll the fish around the stuffing, wrap tightly in foil and bake for 25 minutes or until the fish is cooked.

To serve, slice across the roll. Garnish with tomato pieces.

Angler Baked in Filo

Carol Brendlinger

This wonderful combination of crisp filo, firm fish, mushroom filling and an aromatic tomato sauce was contributed by Carol Brendlinger of Oakland's famed Bay Wolf restaurant.

Alternatives: *Grouper (A,G,P), fancy rockfish   Serves 4*

Duxelles

4 tablespoons butter

½ pound mushrooms, chopped

½ cup chopped shallots

¼ cup cream

½ cup parsley

Salt and pepper to taste

Melt the butter in a skillet. Add the other ingredients and cook over low heat for about 15 minutes.

Tomato Sauce

2 tablespoons olive oil

½ cup chopped shallots

1 teaspoon each fresh thyme, oregano and tarragon or ¼ teaspoon each of dried

1 cup dry white wine

5 large tomatoes, peeled, seeded and chopped

Heat the oil in a heavy saucepan. Add the shallots and herbs. Sauté briefly, add the wine and simmer until the wine is completely evaporated. Add the tomatoes. Simmer for 3 minutes. Set aside until just before the fish is cooked.

Angler in Filo

1 pound angler, cut into 12 ¾-inch slices

2 tablespoons olive oil

¼ pound butter, melted

8 sheets filo pastry (widely available fresh and frozen)

Preheat the oven to 450°
   Sauté the fish in olive oil until it is about two-thirds cooked.

Lay down one sheet of filo. Brush the entire surface lightly with melted butter. Cover it with a second sheet of filo and repeat the brushing. Overlap three pieces of fish at the center of the end of the pastry nearest you. Top with about 2 tablespoons of the *duxelles* mixture. Fold over the two sides of the filo to the center. Brush the folded edges with a little butter to make them stick. Roll up the package and seal it with a little more melted butter. Repeat this procedure for the other three packages. Bake for 10 minutes, or until the pastry is golden brown.

Just before the fish is cooked, reheat the tomato sauce to the simmering point. Spoon it onto a warm serving platter or individual plates. Arrange the pastries on top of the sauce and serve.

Angler Salad

Alternatives: *Lingcod, skate*   *Serves 4 as a first course*

1–1½ tablespoons vinegar

Salt and pepper to taste

⅓–½ cup olive oil

1 pound angler filet, poached and chilled

1 medium red or green bell pepper, seeded and julienned

3–4 scallions, sliced

2 tablespoons or more capers

Leaf lettuce

In a salad bowl, combine the vinegar, salt and pepper. Add the oil, combine thoroughly and correct seasoning. Slice the fish into thin slices or large julienne. Toss the fish in the dressing with the peppers, scallions and capers. Serve on large lettuce leaves.

Warm Cabbage Salad with Angler

Serves 4 as a first course   *Serves 2 as a main course*

4–6 ounces angler filet

1 tablespoon vinegar (sherry, red wine or rice wine)

Large pinch salt

A generous grating of black pepper

4 cups finely shredded red cabbage

1 teaspoon chopped garlic

6 tablespoons olive oil

Have all the ingredients at room temperature.

Cut the angler into crosswise slices or strips about ½ inch thick.

Warm a stainless or other heatproof bowl. Combine the vinegar, salt and pepper in the bowl. Toss the cabbage in this mixture. Correct the seasoning and keep warm.

Sauté the fish pieces and garlic in oil until just done. Pour the hot oil and fish over the cabbage, toss thoroughly and serve on warmed plates.

Angler Stuffing for Pasta

Use this forcemeat to fill ravioli, tortellini and other similar pasta.

Alternatives: *Lingcod, cabezon*   *Yield: Enough for 30–36 ravioli*

1 pound angler filet

Olive oil

1 yellow onion, chopped

1 tablespoon chopped garlic

1 tablespoon chopped parsley

2 tablespoons bread crumbs

½ teaspoon dried thyme or 1½ teaspoons fresh

Salt and pepper to taste

Chop the fish finely with a knife or in a meat grinder or food processor. If using a food processor, be careful not to reduce it to a paste. The chopped fish should be the texture of finely ground beef.

Sauté the onion and garlic in olive oil until soft. Add the remaining ingredients and cook just until the fish loses its raw color. If the fish gives off a large amount of liquid, strain it back into the pan to reduce, adding another teaspoon or so of bread crumbs to absorb the liquid. Add to the stuffing.

Season the mixture to taste, and allow it to cool before filling the pasta.

PACIFIC BARRACUDA

(Sphyraena argentaea)

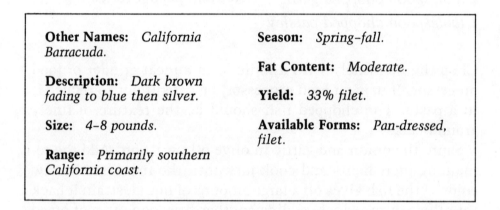

Other Names: *California Barracuda.*

Description: *Dark brown fading to blue then silver.*

Size: *4–8 pounds.*

Range: *Primarily southern California coast.*

Season: *Spring–fall.*

Fat Content: *Moderate.*

Yield: *33% filet.*

Available Forms: *Pan-dressed, filet.*

While the great barracuda *(S. barracuda)* may have toxic flesh, the Pacific variety is perfectly edible and is sporadically available in West Coast markets. Like mahi-mahi, wahoo and other similarly flavored and textured fish, it takes well to grilling and broiling. Serve with a full-flavored sauce such as Wasabi Butter (page 255) or Fresh Tomato Salsa (page 262).

BLACKFISH
(Orodan macrolepododus)

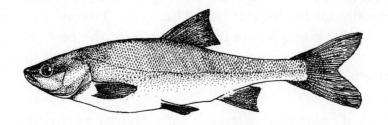

Other Names: *Black trout, Sacramento blackfish, hardhead, Chinese "steelhead."*	*rivers. Has been introduced into southern California where it is aquacultured.*
Description: *Black or dark grey fading to silver. Small scales.*	**Season:** *All year.*
	Fat Content: *Low.*
Size: *2–4 pounds.*	**Yield:** *40% filet.*
Range: *Large lakes and slow-moving brackish waters of the Sacramento and San Joaquin*	**Available Forms:** *Live, round, dressed, pan-dressed.*

Blackfish is the live fish most commonly available in California. It is transported in tank trucks to Chinese markets where it swims in oxygenated water with catfish and carp. Blackfish has a delicate, mild flavor. It is rarely eaten by Caucasians because the Chinese almost never suggest it to their non-Asian customers for fear they will have trouble with the small, fine bones. Care is necessary, but the blackfish is worth it. It is almost always steamed whole.

Steamed Blackfish with Ham

Pork is frequently used as a flavoring in Chinese seafood recipes, especially for freshwater fish. Use a fine-flavored ham such as Smithfield, Westphalian or *prosciutto* for the best results.

Alternatives: *Catfish*   *Serves 4 as a main course*

A 2-pound blackfish, dressed

8 thin slices ginger

8 thin slices ham, 2 inches long by ¾ inch wide

¼ cup loosely packed cilantro

2 tablespoons dry sherry or rice wine

2 tablespoons soy sauce

½ teaspoon white pepper

½ teaspoon cornstarch dissolved in 1 tablespoon water

2 teaspoons sesame oil

Preheat the steamer, which may be a wok with a steaming rack, a stockpot with a perforated insert and a cover, or any other covered vessel which will hold the fish on a plate over the steaming liquid. Be sure to start with plenty of water in the steamer to ensure that it will not boil dry while the fish is cooking.

Extend the belly cavity of the fish by cutting about a third of the way from the vent to the tail, so that the fish will lie flat on the plate. Make four cuts perpendicular to the backbone on either side of the fish. Insert a piece of ginger and a piece of ham into each cut. Place the fish, belly side down, on a plate and surround it with the cilantro. Combine the wine, soy sauce and pepper, pour over the fish and steam until the thickest part of the flesh is done by the skewer test.

Remove the fish to a heated serving platter, draining the sauce into a saucepan. Bring the sauce to a boil and add the cornstarch mixture. As soon as it thickens, pour over the fish, sprinkle with sesame oil and serve.

BONITO

(Sarda chiliensis)

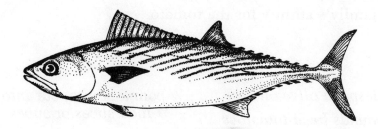

Other Names: *Bonita.*	**Season:** *Late fall–early summer.*
Description: *Steel blue fading to grey. Black oblique stripes.*	**Fat Content:** *Moderate.*
Size: *5 pounds and up.*	**Yield:** *50% filet.*
Range: *Baja to southern California.*	**Available Forms:** *Round, filet.*

One of the most reasonably priced members of the tuna family, bonito is widely available in season. It has a moderate to pronounced flavor and is very easily fileted. The Japanese use dried bonito (in the form of *dashi*) as a basis for soups and sauces. Smaller fish can be used whole in recipes for mackerel, and larger filets or steaks are suitable for any tuna recipe. Bonito makes delicious Ceviche (page 70).

Alternatives: Other tunas, larger mackerel (A,P), yellowtail, other jacks.

Bonito Sauce for Pasta

This is a simple, delicious pasta sauce which illustrates the tuna family's affinity for the tomato.

Serves 2

1 tablespoon olive oil

1½ pounds fresh tomatoes, peeled, seeded and chopped or 2 cups canned tomatoes, chopped

1 shallot, finely chopped or ½ medium yellow onion, finely chopped

1 tablespoon chopped parsley

1 teaspoon fresh thyme or ¼ teaspoon dried thyme

1-2 tablespoons chopped garlic

½ pound bonito, cut into ¾-inch slices or cubes

¼ cup dry white wine

¼ cup concentrated chicken stock (reduce a regular stock by half)

½ pound fresh or dried pasta, such as linguine, tagliarini or spaghetti

A generous grating of black pepper

Salt to taste

In a pot large enough to hold the sauce and the pasta (a wok is ideal), cook the tomatoes, shallot, parsley, thyme and garlic in olive oil until the tomatoes soften. Add the bonito, white wine and chicken stock. Simmer until fish is cooked through. (For fresh pasta, the sauce should be quite liquid. For dried pasta, reduce the sauce further; the dried pasta will not absorb as much liquid.) Correct the seasoning.

Cook the pasta in boiling salted water, drain and toss it in the pot with the sauce.

Serve in heated bowls, with ground black pepper to taste.

Bonito Baked Provençal Style

The combination of flavors is similar to the previous recipe, but here the fish appears as the main ingredient.

Serves 4

2 tablespoons olive oil

1–1½ pounds bonito filets, skin on

4 tomatoes, peeled, seeded and roughly chopped or 1 cup canned tomatoes, chopped

2 teaspoons fresh thyme or ½ teaspoon dried thyme

2–3 canned anchovy filets, rinsed and roughly chopped

12 whole Niçoise or other black olives, pitted and chopped

½ cup dry white wine

Preheat oven to 425°.

Oil a baking dish, preferably one which can be brought to the table. Place the filets in the dish, skin side down. Scatter the rest of the ingredients over the filets. Cover with a lid or seal with aluminum foil. Bake for 15–20 minutes. If there is any excess liquid in the pan, ladle it into a saucepan, reduce and pour over the fish before serving.

Serve the fish from the baking dish, or carefully transfer the filets to a heated serving plate with the tomato sauce on top.

Grilled Bonito with Chinese Soy Marinade

Serves 4

¼ cup soy sauce

2 tablespoons white vinegar

2 tablespoons dry sherry

1 inch ginger, sliced thin

2 teaspoons finely chopped garlic

1 teaspoon cornstarch dissolved in 1 tablespoon water

4 6–8-ounce bonito filets, skin on, from two 1½-pound fish

Cilantro or toasted sesame seeds for garnish

Combine the soy sauce, vinegar, sherry, ginger and garlic. Marinate the filets in the soy mixture for at least 30 minutes in the refrigerator.

Strain the marinade into a small saucepan. Bring to a boil, add the cornstarch mixture and remove from heat as soon as the sauce thickens. Grill the filets skin side up for 2 minutes per side or until just done, basting generously with the sauce.

Serve the bonito accompanied by any remaining sauce, garnished with sprigs of cilantro or toasted sesame seeds.

Stir-Fried Bonito Indonesian Style

Serves 4 as a main dish

1 pound bonito filets, skinned and cut in 1-inch slices

Cornstarch

¼ cup oil

1 medium yellow onion, finely chopped

1 inch ginger, chopped

1–2 tablespoons chopped garlic

2–3 *fresh* serrano, jalapeño or other small hot chiles, seeded and finely chopped

1 tablespoon tamarind paste (page 43) dissolved in 3 tablespoons water

2 tablespoons white vinegar

2 tablespoons water or chicken stock

2 teaspoons soy sauce

2 teaspoons sugar

Cilantro for garnish

Dust the bonito lightly with cornstarch.

Fry the fish in hot oil. When brown, remove the pieces from the pan. Pour off all but 2 tablespoons of the oil. Add the onions, ginger, garlic and chiles. Sauté until the onions are transparent. Add the tamarind mixture, vinegar, water or stock, soy sauce and sugar. Cook for 1 minute, stirring frequently. Return the bonito to the pan for a few seconds until reheated.

Garnish with cilantro and serve with rice.

Ceviche

Many people think of this Latin American standard as raw fish. "Cold-cooked" would be a better description. The lime juice "cooks" the seafood, transforming the protein in the same way that heating it does. This preparation can be used for almost any saltwater shellfish or fish (an exception is salmon—see An Ounce of Prevention, page 281).

Alternatives: *Rockfish, halibut, scallops, oysters, whelk, abalone*

Serves 4 as an appetizer

½ pound of bonito filets, cut into 1-inch cubes

Lime juice to cover the fish, approximately ¼ cup

1 or 2 fresh serrano, Fresno or other hot chiles, seeded and chopped

2 tablespoons chopped cilantro

1 tomato, peeled, seeded and chopped

Salt to taste

Thin slices of red onion or scallion for garnish

In a small stainless or glass bowl, combine the fish, chiles and cilantro. Cover with lime juice, tossing the fish to moisten pieces evenly. Cover and refrigerate at least 1 hour. Fifteen minutes before serving, add tomato and salt to taste. Garnish with onion or scallion slices.

Ceviche can be served in glasses, on a bed of greens or in avocado halves.

BUFFALOFISH

(Ictiobus cyprinellus)

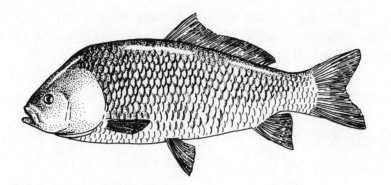

Other Names: *Lake buffalo, blue buffalo, bigmouth buffalo.*	**Season:** *All year.*
	Fat Content: *Moderate.*
Description: *Dark brown or blue fading to pale olive.*	**Yield:** *25% filet.*
Size: *3–12 pounds.*	**Available Forms:** *Live, round, pan-dressed, halved, filet.*
Range: *Rivers and lakes of north-central and south-central United States.*	

A favorite in the South, buffalofish is sold in markets which cater to lovers of freshwater fish. It is frequently available live, especially in Chinese fish markets. The meat has a firm texture and a mild, sweet flavor.

Baked Buffalofish with Creole Sauce

Creole sauce has come to mean just about anything with tomatoes and cayenne. Without making any claims to authenticity, we think this is a very good version.

Alternatives: *Grouper (A,G,P), snapper (A,G), lingcod, rockfish*   *Serves 4*

1 tablespoon olive oil

1 tablespoon butter

1 small yellow onion, julienned

2 small bell peppers, roasted, peeled and julienned

3 scallions, chopped

4-6 cloves garlic, chopped

2 medium tomatoes, peeled, seeded and chopped, juice reserved or 1 small can peeled tomatoes with juice

1 bay leaf

1 teaspoon capers

¼ cup green sliced green olives

½ teaspoon paprika

Cayenne to taste

Zest of 1 lemon

¼ cup dry white wine

1-1½ pounds buffalofish filet

Sauté the vegetables in oil and butter until soft but not browned. Add all but the fish and simmer for at least 30 minutes; the flavor will improve with up to 3 hours of slow cooking. Correct the seasoning.

Preheat oven to 400°.

Place the fish in a deep baking dish or ovenproof casserole and cover with the sauce. Bake with lid on for 12–15 minutes.

Serve over rice with Tabasco or another hot sauce on the side.

PACIFIC BUTTERFISH

(Peprilus simillimus)

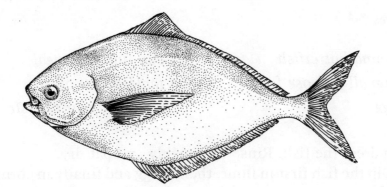

Other Names: *California pompano.*	**Season:** *Spring and summer.*
Description: *Metallic silver, greenish above. No scales.*	**Fat Content:** *Moderate.*
	Yield: *60–70% pan-dressed.*
Size: *Under 1 pound.*	**Available Forms:** *Round.*
Range: *Pacific coast, primarily southern California.*	

There is no unambiguous name for this fish. It is not related to the Florida pompano or to the Pacific sablefish (a fish generally marketed as butterfish in West Coast markets). Whatever you choose to call it, this fish has moderately flavored, soft flesh that is best suited to dry-heat cooking in a batter. Its tender skin will not survive either grilling or sautéing without a coating.

Pan-Fried Butterfish

Serves 2–3

1 pound butterfish	*1 cup fine cornmeal*
1 cup all-purpose flour	*4 tablespoons oil*
1 egg	*Salt and pepper to taste*

Pan-dress the fish. Rinse thoroughly and pat dry.

Dip the fish first in flour, then in egg and finally in cornmeal. Shake off any excess meal. Fry in the oil until golden brown. Turn and brown the other side.

Serve with lemon wedges and Tartar Sauce (page 259).

CABEZON
(Scorpaenichthys marmoratus)

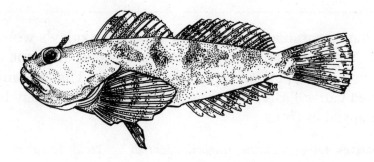

Description: *Variable. Mottled green to red.*	**Season:** *All year.*
Size: *3–10 pounds.*	**Fat Content:** *Low.*
	Yield: *20% filet.*
Range: *Baja to Alaska.*	**Available Forms:** *Round, filet.*

A commercial fish of minor importance, cabezon is the largest member of the sculpin family. It is frequently caught by sport fishermen.

The flesh of cabezon is fairly firm and mild in flavor, and can to be used in much the same way as angler. The roe of cabezon is poisonous.

Thai Fish Cakes
Somchai Aksomboon

Somchai Aksomboon, owner and chef of Berkeley's wonderful Siam Cuisine restaurant, provided this recipe. It is one of the most popular appetizers in many American Thai restaurants. The Red Curry Paste, which is the key ingredient, may be prepared ahead of time.

Alternatives: *Other sculpins, lingcod, rockfish*   *Yield: 18 cakes*

1 pound of cabezon filets, cut into 1-inch slices

1½ tablespoons Red Curry Paste (page 266)

1 tablespoon fish sauce (page 40)

¼ cup string beans, thinly sliced crosswise

Oil for frying

Thai Sweet and Sour Dipping Sauce (see below)

Chop the fish in a food processor or grind finely in a meat grinder. In a bowl, mix the fish together with the curry paste and fish sauce. Add the string beans and combine.

Heat oil to 350°. Form the fish mixture into cakes about ½ inch thick and 2 inches in diameter. Fry the cakes until dark brown, but not burnt. They are done when they float to the top. Serve with the following sauce.

Thai Sweet and Sour Dipping Sauce

¼ cup white wine vinegar

¼ cup sugar

Scant ½ teaspoon salt

2 tablespoons cucumber, peeled and cut into ¼-inch dice

2 teaspoons roughly chopped roasted peanuts

1 jalapeño or other medium hot fresh chile, chopped

Combine the vinegar, sugar and salt in a saucepan. Bring to a boil, remove from the heat and allow to cool. Just before serving, add the cucumber, peanuts and chile.

CARP

(Cyprinus carpio)

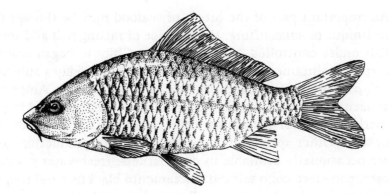

Description: *Gold to olive brown fading to pale yellow. Red highlights. Coarse scales.*	**Season:** *All year.*
	Fat Content: *Moderate.*
Size: *2–3 pounds.*	**Yield:** *25% boneless meat.*
Range: *Aquacultured in many states.*	**Available Forms:** *Live, pan-dressed, chunk.*

Carp was the first fish to be aquacultured, some 2500 years ago in China. Because it is easily raised, this species will become more important here as a food fish in the years to come. Carp is primarily associated with Asian and central European recipes but it is actually one of the most versatile freshwater fish. Its flaky, white, mild-flavored flesh is ideal for frying, baking in a sauce or braising, especially in combination with other freshwater fish such as catfish and eel.

Aquaculture

An important part of the future of seafood may be the age-old technique of *aquaculture*, the practice of raising fish and shellfish under controlled conditions. The Chinese began rearing carp in maintained ponds 2500 years ago, and today a substantial part of the fish eaten in Asia is aquacultured. American aquaculturists are responsible for most of the trout sold in our markets, and for increasing amounts of catfish, crayfish and oysters. Other species are coming into major production, and are occasionally available in our markets: freshwater prawns, carp, pan-sized coho salmon, Sacramento blackfish and tilapia, an introduced Asian species. Research is under way on aquaculture of American lobster, striped bass, sturgeon, abalone and clams.

Aquaculture includes a variety of techniques, from simple protection and maintenance of oyster beds to total artificial environments. All methods, however, have the common aim of increased food yield per acre of water. Publicists and popular writers like to describe a rosy future for aquaculture, with 6- to 8-fold production increases over the next 20 years. Still, aquaculture is not without its problems, both economic and technological. Competition for water and land is stiff; also, water is a difficult growing medium to manage, as disease organisms can spread rapidly through dense populations of fish and shellfish.

Still, aquaculture will play a growing role in supplying seafood for Americans and the rest of the world. In addition to broadening the range of choices of seafood, aquaculture can reduce the dependence on certain overfished wild stocks, and in some cases help to replenish wild populations.

Sweet and Sour Fish

Bruce Cost

Bruce Cost teaches Chinese cooking, having studied for many years with Virginia Lee, a leading authority on Chinese food. Many of his recipes come from the Shanghai region, which favors rich, complex sauces. Bruce is currently working on a ginger cookbook.

Alternatives: *Fancy rockfish, black sea bass (A), striped bass (A,G,P)*

Serves 6 or more as a side dish
Serves 2–3 as a main course

A 2–2½-pound carp, dressed

1 egg, beaten

Salt

½ cup cornstarch

4 dried black mushrooms (the common Chinese variety)

1 small yellow onion, peeled and cut into quarters

3 thin slices ginger

5 cloves garlic, cracked and peeled

2 fresh red sweet or hot peppers, cut into 1-inch dice

2 scallions, cut into 1-inch lengths and then shredded lengthwise

6 pickled shallots or pickled scallions (available in Asian groceries)

1½ cups water

¾ cup sugar

½ cup red wine vinegar

2 teaspoons dark soy sauce

2 teaspoons light soy sauce

1 teaspoon salt

2½ tablespoons cornstarch dissolved in ¼ cup water

Oil for frying

Cilantro for garnish

Extend the belly cavity from the vent almost to the fin. Place the fish belly side down on the cutting board. Press down hard on top of the head of the fish with the heel of your hand to crack the head open. The fish can then be cooked and served in an upright position. Make deep diagonal cuts almost to the backbone at 1-inch intervals from gill openings to tail.

Blend the egg and salt. Rub this mixture over the fish and into the cut surfaces. Spoon a couple of tablespoons of cornstarch into a sieve and sift it over the fish. Rub it in well and let it stand for 15 minutes. Repeat this procedure 3 or 4 times, rubbing in the cornstarch each time.

Meanwhile, soak the mushrooms in hot water for 15 minutes. Drain, squeezing to extract the moisture. Cut off and discard the stems. Cut the caps in two and set aside in a mixing bowl with the onion, ginger, garlic, peppers, scallions and pickled shallots.

Combine water, sugar, vinegar, soy sauces and salt in a saucepan and bring to a boil, stirring to dissolve the sugar; lower the temperature and keep warm.

Heat oil to near smoking (400°) in a large wok or heavy pot. Cook fish over high heat for 10–15 minutes. The fish should be golden-brown but still adhere well to the bones. Drain off the excess oil and place on a large platter. (The fish may be cooked to this point several hours ahead. Just before you are ready to serve, fry the fish again, cooking for about 5 minutes, drain and place on a large platter.)

Heat ¼ cup of oil in a wok or skillet and add the mushrooms and other reserved vegetables. Stir fry for 1 minute then add the sugar/vinegar mixture. Bring to a boil. Add the cornstarch mixture and cook until clear. Pour the sauce over the fish and serve, garnished with cilantro.

CATFISH
(Ictalurus punctatus)

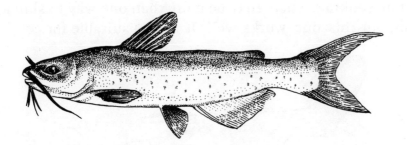

Other Names: *Channel catfish.*	**Season:** *All year.*
Description: *Dark grey fading to white. Irregular black spots.*	**Fat Content:** *Moderate.*
	Yield: *50% filet.*
Size: *1–3 pounds. Larger in the wild.*	**Available Forms:** *Live, round, pan-dressed, filet.*
Range: *Widespread throughout North America. Aquacultured in many states.*	

Without a doubt, catfish is one of the fish of the future. Tens of millions of pounds are grown annually, yet the supply falls short of the rapidly growing demand. Catfish take well to aquaculture, adapting easily to crowded conditions as long as the water is clean and well oxygenated.

Until recently, cultural prejudice has kept many Americans from trying catfish which has traditionally been thought of as a "trash fish." Now, however, catfish is being consumed outside its narrow regional and ethnic market as more people discover its fine cooking qualities.

Catfish has a flaky, moist texture and a mild, agreeable fresh-water flavor. It is well-suited to frying, sautéing, steaming or braising.

Alternatives: *Blackfish.*

To Skin a Catfish

Because of the toughness of its skin, catfish must be skinned before cooking. There may be more than one way to skin a catfish, but this one works well. It is also suitable for eel.

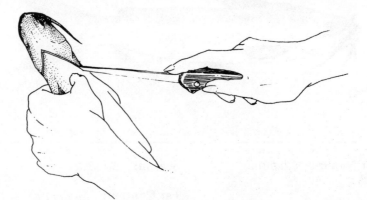

1 Make a V-shaped incision just through the skin, starting from the top of the head and down behind the operculum.

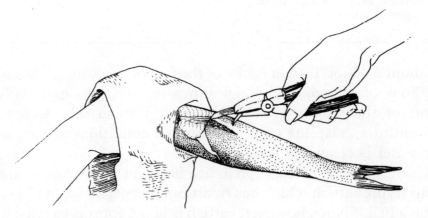

2 Wearing a glove or using a towel to protect your hand from the barbed "whiskers," hold the fish by the head, grasp a flap of skin with pliers and pull the skin away towards the tail. (A helpful device, if you have many catfish or eels to skin, is a board with an exposed nail protruding from one end; impale the fish head on the nail to hold the fish while you pull the skin off.)

Catfish in Red Curry Sauce

Somchai Aksomboon

Alternatives: *Rockfish, tilefish (A), grouper (A,G,P)*

Serves 4 as a side dish
Serves 2 as a main course

2 tablespoons Red Curry
  Paste (page 266)

4 tablespoons oil

2 cups coconut milk
  (page 39)

½ teaspoon salt

1 teaspoon sugar

3 tablespoons fish sauce
  (page 40)

A 2-pound pan-dressed
  catfish, cut into 1-inch
  steaks

1 tablespoon Thai basil
  leaves or substitute Italian
  basil and mint leaves

1–3 fresh hot chiles, finely
  chopped

Heat the curry paste in oil. Stir and cook for 2 minutes. Add ¼ cup of the coconut milk and the fish sauce. Simmer slowly for 2 minutes to release the flavor of the curry. Then add salt, sugar and the rest of the coconut milk. Bring to a boil and as soon as the sauce boils, add the fish. Do not stir the fish until the sauce returns to a boil. Chai, who likes his fish without even a hint of a fishy taste, says that if you disturb the fish before the sauce boils, it will acquire a strong aroma. Simmer the fish until done, about 5 minutes. Let the dish sit for at least 15 minutes (or as long as overnight in the refrigerator) so the curry flavor will permeate the fish. Reheat, without boiling. Just before serving, add the basil leaves and chiles. Serve over rice.

Fried Catfish Chinese Style

The Chinese love catfish, which they prefer to buy live. In Hong Kong, many restaurants have tanks full of swimming catfish. This practice has been transplanted to America where certain Cantonese fish markets and restaurants offer live catfish.

Serves 4

¼ cup dry sherry or rice wine

½ teaspoon five spice powder (page 40)

1 pound catfish filets

1 egg white

2 tablespoons cornstarch

1 cup white sesame seeds

Peanut oil for frying

Marinate the filets for 30 minutes in the sherry and five spice powder. Beat the egg white and cornstarch together. Dip filets into the egg mixture, then coat with sesame seeds.

Heat the oil to 350° in a wok or deep-fryer. Fry the filets until golden brown. Drain on paper towels.

Serve with Green Chile Sauce (page 264) or Fresh Cilantro Chutney (page 265).

Fried Catfish Southern Style

To minimize the slight freshwater flavor of catfish, soak the filets in buttermilk for 15 minutes or more. Drain slightly. Roll the filets, still wet with the buttermilk, in seasoned cornmeal until well coated. Fry or pan-fry the filets in butter, oil or bacon drippings until golden brown. Serve with lemon wedges and Tartar Sauce (page 259) or Creole Mayonnaise (page 257). Fried catfish is traditionally served with hush puppies which are small sticks of fried cornbread batter.

Laotian Catfish Soup

This is a recipe from *Traditional Dishes of Laos* by Phia Sing (Prospect Books, London, distributed by the University Press of Virginia). Laotian food is almost unknown in America although quite a few of the recent immigrants from Asia come from Laos. Laos is landlocked but rich in freshwater aquatic life. As is the case throughout Southeast Asia, catfish is an important Laotian food source.

Serves 4 as a first course

1 fresh jalapeño or *Fresno* chile, seeded

1 small Japanese-style eggplant

3 shallots, unpeeled

1 whole head of garlic

3 cups chicken stock or water

½ pound catfish filets, cut into 1-inch squares

Juice of 1 lime

1–2 teaspoons fish sauce (page 40)

½ cucumber, peeled, seeded and cut into ½-inch dice

Finely chopped cilantro

Lime wedges for garnish

Grill the chiles, eggplant, shallots and garlic over a fire or under the broiler. When they are nicely browned, remove their skins and pound them together in a mortar or purée in a food processor.

Poach the fish in the chicken stock until cooked. Remove to individual warmed bowls. Stir the puréed vegetables into the poaching liquid. Bring to a boil and remove from the heat. Add lime juice, fish sauce, cilantro and cucumber to the soup. Ladle the liquid over the fish. Serve immediately, accompanied with lime wedges.

Thai Sour Fish Soup

Somchai Aksomboon

Alternatives: *Cheap rockfish, sablefish, sculpin*   *Serves 4 as a first course*

4 shallots, peeled and left whole

1 stalk fresh lemongrass or 1 teaspoon dried lemongrass, finely chopped

1 quart water

1 teaspoon peppercorns

2 tablespoons fish sauce (page 40)

2 tablespoons cilantro

1½ teaspoon tamarind paste (page 43) dissolved in 2 tablespoons water

½ teaspoon shrimp paste (page 43) (optional)

¼ pound catfish filets, cut into 1-inch slices

Cilantro for garnish

Simmer 3 of the shallots and the lemongrass in the water for 10 minutes. In the meantime, pound the other shallot, the cilantro and the peppercorns in a mortar. Add this paste, the fish sauce, the tamarind mixture and the optional shrimp paste to the soup stock. Simmer for 10 minutes. Add the fish slices and cook until done. Serve immediately, garnished with cilantro.

CLAM—HARD-SHELL

Pacific Littleneck

(Prothaca staminea)

Other Names: *Rock clam, painted clam.*	**Season:** *All year. Better in colder months.*
Description: *Similar to Atlantic hard-shell, but smaller in size.*	**Fat Content:** *Low.*
	Yield: *25% meat.*
Size: *Average 10 per pound.*	**Available Forms:** *Live, smoked.*
Range: *Humboldt Bay to Alaska. Commercially harvested from the California-Oregon border north.*	**Similar Species:** *Manila clam* (Tapes phillippinarium), *is a dark, triangular shaped clam, running about 15 per pound.*

Atlantic

(Mercenaria mercenaria)

Other Names: *Littleneck, cherrystone, quahag or quahog are market terms for the same species. Littleneck are the smallest, quahag the largest.*	*commercial grounds are in southern New England.*
	Season: *All year. Better in colder months.*
Description: *Bivalve. Chalky grey to manila brown.*	**Fat Content:** *Low.*
Size: *12 per pound to 1 per pound.*	**Yield:** *15–30% meat. Better yield from smaller clams.*
Range: *Atlantic coast. Main*	**Available Forms:** *Live, shucked, smoked.*

The hard-shell clam species mentioned above are representative of hundreds of closely related species which are often mixed together and sold under a variety of names.

Eastern hard-shells are usually shucked and eaten on the half-shell; western varieties are tougher and not as well suited to this treatment. Clams should be cooked as little as possible as they quickly become tough. (There are always a few stubborn clams in each batch which refuse to open quickly. To avoid overcooking the others, remove clams as they open. The stubborn ones may also be opened with a knife, but away from the pot as the shells might be full of mud.) Hard-shell clams can be steamed, braised or grilled in the shell. Once opened, they can be stuffed. Any of the mussel recipes in this book are appropriate for hard-shell clams.

To Shuck a Clam

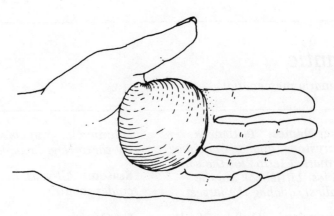

1 Hold the clam securely in the palm of your left hand, with the notched side toward your thumb. Work over a bowl to catch spilled juices.

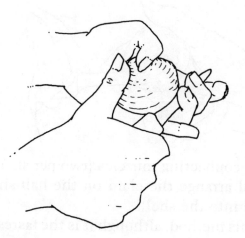

2 Position the thin edge of a *clam knife* (page 18) or a sturdy but slightly dull paring knife along the seam between the two shells. Squeezing with the fingers of your left hand, force the knife between the shells.

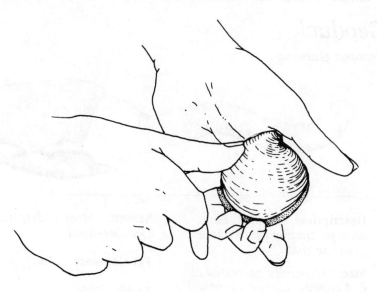

3 Continue working the knife between the shells towards the hinge until you can pry the shells apart.

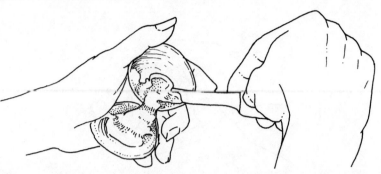

4 Sever the connecting muscles (two per shell), separate the shells and arrange the clam on the half-shell. Spoon any reserved juice into the shell.

Note that this method, although it is the fastest, cuts through part of the clam meat. If you wish to keep the meat intact, carefully work the tip of the knife up against the inside of the upper shell before separating the shells.

CLAM—SOFT-SHELL

(This accepted description is somewhat misleading; the shells of these species are actually thin and brittle, not soft.)

Geoduck

(Panopea generosa)

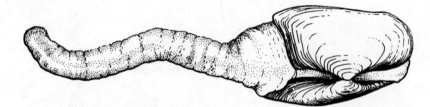

Description: *Bivalve. Large neck protruding up to a foot from the shell.*

Size: *Generally harvested at 2-4 pounds. Largest intertidal mollusc.*

Range: *Washington and British Columbia.*

Season: *Most widely available October–April.*

Fat Content: *Low.*

Yield: *70%.*

Available Forms: *Live.*

Geoduck (pronounced gooey-duck) is delicious raw as *sashimi* or marinated in Ceviche (page 70). Sliced, pounded and sautéed, it resembles abalone. It also makes a wonderful chowder.

To Clean a Geoduck

Remove it from the shell with a knife. Dip the neck into hot water for 30 seconds and peel back the skin. Cut away and discard the entrails. Slice diagonally into thin strips.

Other Soft-Shell Clams

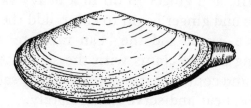

Steamer clams *(Mya arenaria)* of the East Coast are sometimes available on the West Coast. They can be steamed in the shell or shucked and sautéed, and are delicious marinated in a vinaigrette dressing.

Razor clams *(Siliqua patula*—Pacific species; *Enis directus*—Atlantic species) are primarily sport species. Long and narrow, they resemble a folded straight razor. Treat them as you would steamer clams.

Clams in Black Bean Sauce

Bruce Cost

Serves 6 or more as a side dish

2 tablespoons salted black
   beans (page 42)

2 tablespoons dry sherry or
   rice wine

3 tablespoons oil

1 tablespoon chopped garlic

2 teaspoons chopped ginger

4 pounds hard-shell clams,
   in the shell

Serves 4 as a main course

½ cup clam broth

½ teaspoon soy sauce

1 teaspoon sugar

1 teaspoon cornstarch
   dissolved in 1 tablespoon
   water

Coarsely chop the beans and soak them in the sherry for at least
30 minutes.

Steam the clams open and reserve the broth.

Sauté the garlic and ginger in oil in a heavy skillet or wok.
When the garlic and ginger begin to color, add the clams, clam
broth, soy sauce, sugar and the bean mixture. Stir-fry for 2
minutes, coating all the clams with the sauce. Add the cornstarch mixture and continue stirring. When the sauce thickens,
remove from the heat and serve immediately.

Clams with Lemon in Oyster Sauce

Bruce Cost

Lemon peel is a fairly common ingredient in Cantonese cooking although it is not often seen in American-style Cantonese dishes.

Serves 4 as a side dish   *Serves 2 as a main course*

24 medium clams

2 cups water

1 tablespoon shredded ginger

2 small fresh hot chiles, shredded

1 tablespoon shredded lemon peel

1 tablespoon grated lemon peel

1 tablespoon salted black beans (page 42)

2-4 cloves garlic, chopped

1 tablespoon dry sherry

1 tablespoon soy sauce

2 tablespoons Chinese oyster sauce

1 teaspoon sugar

4 tablespoons oil

1 tablespoon cornstarch mixed with 3 tablespoons water

Cilantro for garnish

Scrub the clams.

Bring 2 cups of water to a boil in a wok or large pot. Add the clams, cover and steam just until they open. Immediately remove them to a bowl filled with ice water to stop the cooking. Save the clam broth. Drain the clams.

Combine the ginger, hot chiles and the shredded lemon peel.

Chop the black beans and combine with the garlic and sherry.

Combine the reserved clam stock, soy sauce, oyster sauce, grated lemon peel and sugar.

Heat the oil in a wok or large skillet. Add the ginger mixture, stir 10 seconds and add the black bean mixture. Cook 30 seconds and add the clam stock-soy sauce mixture. When the sauce boils, add the cornstarch mixture. Cook until thickened, then add the clams. Stir until clams are heated and coated with the sauce. Serve the clams in their shells with the sauce. Garnish with cilantro.

Clam Sauce for Pasta

Although this dish is delicious with any pasta, the thinner cuts such as linguine or tagliarini are most suited to seafood sauces. Of course, fresh pasta is preferable to the dried variety.

Serves 4 as a first course   *Serves 2 as a main course*

2 pounds clams

½ cup white wine

1 tablespoon or more
  chopped garlic

2 tablespoons butter

1 tablespoon chopped parsley

½ pound fresh or dried pasta

Salt and pepper to taste

Combine all ingredients except pasta in a skillet with a tight lid. Cover, bring to a boil and steam until clams open. Meanwhile, cook the pasta, drain well and toss with the clam sauce.

Serve in shallow bowls with clams arranged on top in their shells. Sprinkle with additional chopped parsley, if desired.

PACIFIC COD

(Gadus macrocephalus)

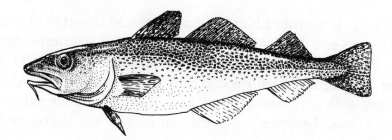

Other Names: *True cod.*	**Season:** *All year.*
Description: *Brown or grey with browish spots above. Paler below.*	**Fat Content:** *Low.*
	Yield: *40% filet.*
Size: *5–10 pounds.*	**Available Forms:** *Filet.*
Range: *Oregon to Bering Sea.*	

This is the only true Pacific representative of the cod family. Rock cod, lingcod and black cod are all local names for unrelated species. For this reason, this species is often marketed here as "true cod." It is nearly identical to the Atlantic variety, with only minor anatomical differences.

Cod, with its white, flaky, very mild flesh, is a versatile food fish, suitable for grilling, broiling, frying, baking, poaching and stewing. It may be freely substituted in recipes for rockfish, lingcod, sablefish or any other mild-flavored white fish.

Fish Chowder with Leeks

This recipe is neither a New England nor a Manhattan chowder. If leeks are not available, the white parts of scallions may be used; yellow onions are not a good substitute. Although this recipe is recommended for cod, any mild, lean white fish will do. Very soft varieties such as sablefish or smaller soles will more or less disappear into the soup, and are therefore less desirable.

Alternatives: *Rockfish, sculpin, lingcod, halibut, larger flatfish*

Serves 8

2 tablespoons butter

½ cup thinly sliced leeks (the white and pale green parts—save the tops for stock)

2 large (about 1 pound) new potatoes, scrubbed or peeled, cut into ½-inch dice

1 quart Fumet (page 252)

2 cups milk or half-and-half

1 pound cod filets cut in bite-sized pieces

Salt and pepper to taste

2 tablespoons chopped parsley or 1 tablespoon chervil

In a large saucepan, melt the butter and cook the leeks gently until soft, about 5 minutes. Add the potatoes and liquids, bring to a boil and simmer until potatoes are tender, about 15 minutes. Add the fish and simmer just until it is done; remember that the fish will continue to cook in the soup, even when removed from the heat.

Season to taste with salt and pepper. Just before serving, stir in the herbs. Serve in shallow soup bowls with a good crusty bread.

CORBINA

(Menticirrhus undulatus)

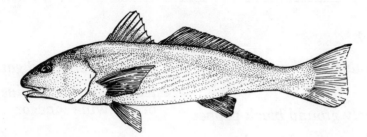

Other Names: *Corvina.*	**Season:** *Spring–summer.*
Description: *Uniform metallic grey with gold highlights.*	**Fat Content:** *Moderate.*
	Yield: *33% filet.*
Size: *3–7 pounds.*	**Available Forms:** *Round, pan-dressed, filet.*
Range: *Southern California and Baja California coasts.*	

This small West Coast representative of the croaker family has firm, fairly rich flesh with a moderately pronounced flavor. It is well suited to grilling, broiling and steaming.

Alternatives: *Seabass (P), striped bass (A,P), drum, redfish, sea trout, snapper, grouper (A,G).*

Sautéed Corbina with Piquant Sauce

Serves 4

1½ pounds corbina filet	*1 teaspoon chopped garlic*
Salt	*2 teaspoons sherry vinegar*
Coarsely ground black pepper	*or red wine vinegar*
2 tablespoons olive oil	

Cut the filet into 4 serving pieces. Season with a little salt and a generous amount of pepper. In a large skillet, sauté the fish in olive oil over moderate to high heat until done. Transfer the filets to a heated serving platter or individual plates. Sauté the garlic in the remaining oil, but do not brown. Off the heat, add the vinegar (carefully—it will splatter). Return to the heat for a few seconds to evaporate some of the vinegar and pour the sauce over the fish.

Serve with steamed or boiled new potatoes with butter and parsley.

Corbina Steamed in Lettuce

This is one of the best uses for iceberg lettuce.

Serves 4 or more as a first course   *Serves 2 as a main dish*

¾ pound corbina filet

2 tablespoons soy sauce

2 tablespoons dry sherry

6–8 slices ginger

1–2 cloves garlic, chopped

Outer leaves of iceberg or
  butter lettuce (see below)

Slice the filet across the grain into 1-ounce pieces. Marinate the fish pieces in the soy sauce, sherry, ginger and garlic for 30 minutes.

Peel off enough lettuce leaves to wrap the fish pieces, tearing the large leaves into several pieces if necessary. Blanch the leaves in rapidly boiling water for a few seconds and rinse them in cold water and drain. Wrap each piece of fish in a leaf, forming a tight envelope. Steam on a plate with any remaining marinade until the fish is done, about 5–8 minutes.

CRAB

Dungeness Crab

(Cancer magister)

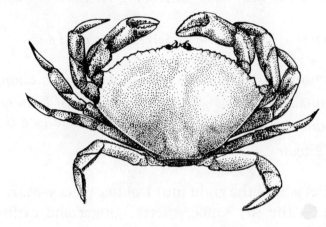

Other Names: *Market crab, common crab.*	**Season:** *October–May.*
Description: *Reddish brown to purple above, cream to yellow below when raw. Brick red to orange when cooked.*	**Fat Content:** *Low (in meat).*
	Yield: *25% meat.*
	Available Forms: *Live, cooked, fresh meat.*
Size: *1½–3 pounds and up.*	
Range: *Baja California to Alaska. Most common from central California north.*	

This is the main commercial crab on the West Coast, and is a symbol to many of Fisherman's Wharf in San Francisco. Much of the catch is frozen for sale in the off season.

The Dungeness crab population seems to fluctuate on a cycle of about seven years. A large population supports the growth of a parasite which feeds on the crab's eggs. Peak populations of the parasite follow crab peaks by several years, reducing the crab population until the egg supply in turn diminishes and cannot support the parasite population.

Blue Crab

(Callinectes sapidus)

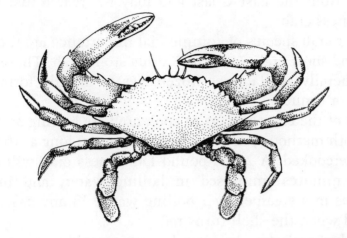

Other Names: *Soft-shell crab.*

Description: *Dark blue to dark green with blue or cream mottling above, cream below. Light to dark orange above, white below when cooked.*

Size: *3½–7 inches across, 2 per pound hard-shell, 4–6 per pound soft-shell.*

Range: *South Atlantic coast to New Jersey; Gulf of Mexico.*

Season: *All year, local seasons depend on water temperature.*

Fat Content: *Low (in meat).*

Yield: *20% meat from hard-shell.*

Available Forms: *Live, picked or lump meat.*

The blue crab is the major commercial species on the Atlantic and Gulf coasts and is second only to shrimp in volume of the catch.

As this crab grows, it periodically sheds its shell to grow a larger one. In this stage it is known as a soft-shell, and is especially good eating. Experienced crabbers can spot ''busters,'' or crabs about to molt, and keep them apart from the rest of the catch. As soon as the crab has shed its shell, it must be transferred immediately to fresh water or it will begin to harden.

Soft-shell blue crabs are widely available frozen, and occasionally appear fresh in our area. Soft-shells are usually fried, sautéed or broiled, and the whole crab is eaten, soft outer layer and all. Hard-shell blue crabs are also available live by air freight from the East Coast and may be treated just like the Dungeness crab.

Other crab species of commercial importance are the Alaska king and snow crabs, and the Florida stone crab. These species are generally available as frozen legs or in bulk form, either frozen or canned.

Two of the easiest ways to cook crab are boiling and steaming. Both methods yield moist, firm meat as long as the crab is not overcooked. A 2–2½-pound Dungeness crab will cook in 10–12 minutes immersed in boiling water, and in 12–15 minutes in a steamer over boiling water. In any case, crab is cooked when the shell turns red.

Cracked crab may be served warm or cold. For warm crab, serve with a hot butter sauce such as Lemon-Garlic Butter (page 255), or with one of the chutneys or dipping sauces on pages 264–65. Cold crab is best with one of the mayonnaise sauces, especially Creole Mayonnaise (page 258).

For an attractive presentation of whole crab, arrange the legs and claws in a lifelike pattern around the body meat, and cover the body with the shell.

To Clean a Cooked Dungeness Crab

No matter how you intend to serve a cooked crab, the cleaning procedure is the same.

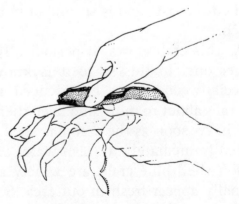

1 Hold the crab from underneath. Grasp the top shell by the edges and pull it up and away from the body. Do not discard the shell.

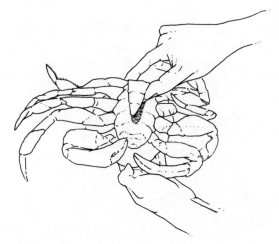

2 Turn the crab over. Lift the "breastplate," a roughly tri-
angular piece of shell, being careful of the soft spines hid-
den underneath. Remove these together with the breastplate,
and discard.

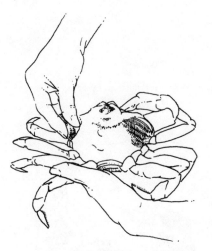

3 Looking at the upper side of the crab again, remove and discard the gills ("dead men's fingers") on either side of the
body above the legs. Remove and discard the intestine, a firm
white crooked piece along the center of the back.

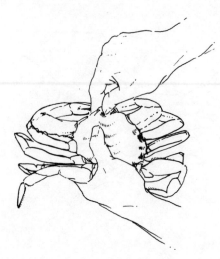

4 Remove and discard the mouth parts. The body cavity will be full of a soft, white to yellow mass of fat and edible organs collectively known as "butter." This is a delicious and essential ingredient in many crab dishes. Remove and reserve the butter. Rinse any remaining matter from the body of the crab, which should now be just shell and meat.

5 Reach into the corners of the shell for any more butter. Rinse the shell if it is to be used in presentation.

To Crack a Cooked and Cleaned Dungeness Crab

Cracking the crab in the kitchen prior to serving makes eating the crab an easier and less messy business at the table. The legs may be separated from the body, which is then served whole or in halves; alternatively, the body may be cut into pieces, each attached to a leg, as shown on page 107.

1 To remove the legs, hold the body, grasp each leg as close to the body as possible, and twist to separate the leg from the body.

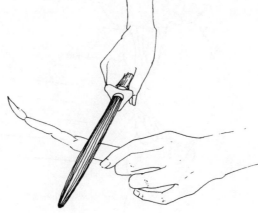

2 Crack each leg and claw section with a mallet, a sharpening steel or the back of a heavy cleaver, being careful not to mash the meat inside.

To Kill and Clean a Crab

Use this technique for grilling, stir-frying or any other method where precooked crab is not appropriate. Refrigerate the live crab for several hours before preparing it to render it a bit more docile.

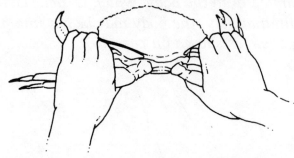

1 Approach the crab from behind. Grasp all four legs and the claw on each side near the body, being careful to avoid the powerful claws.

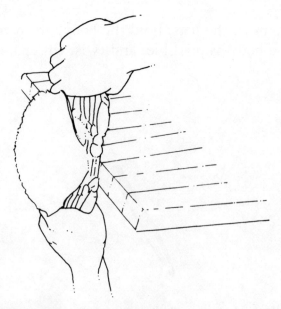

2 Using a sharp edge of a sink, tabletop or cutting board, crack the underside of the shell down the middle with one sharp blow, stunning the crab.

107

3 Draw both sets of legs together in one hand, grasp the shell with the other hand and pull the body out of the shell. The crab may now be cleaned by the same method for a cooked crab.

4 Or, if the crab is less lively and the shell is not being used for presentation, the crab may be split with a knife, shell and all, and cleaned by the same method.

5 **For Sautéing or Stir-Frying:** Cut each half of the body into sections with each section attached to a leg. Crack each leg before cooking.

6 **For Grilling:** Leave the crab halves intact or partially split; crack the legs before marinating, while still attached.

Grilled Crab

Serves 2

1 inch thinly sliced ginger
¼ cup olive oil
1 tablespoon chopped garlic
1 tablespoon chopped parsley
½ teaspoon coarsely ground
 black pepper

2 serrano or other hot green
 chiles, chopped
1 2-2½-pound live crab,
 halved and cracked
¼ cup butter

Combine the ginger, oil, garlic, parsley, black pepper and chiles in a bowl. Add the crab pieces. Toss and refrigerate for at least 1 hour. Strain the marinade, reserving the vegetables for the dipping sauce and the liquid for basting the crab. Grill the crab 3–4 minutes per side, depending on the heat of the fire. Baste with the marinade liquid. Meanwhile, melt the butter in a saucepan. Add the reserved vegetables. Simmer for 5 minutes. Serve with the crab.

Green Crab Enchiladas

Serves 4 (8 enchiladas)

1 pound tomatillos, *husks removed, or 1 large can of* tomatillos, *drained (page 44)*

2 tablespoons oil

4 serrano, *Fresno or other hot fresh chiles, seeded and finely chopped*

1–2 tablespoons chopped garlic

¼ cup chopped cilantro

2 cups crab meat, *(about 1 pound)*

8 corn tortillas

Oil for frying (about ⅛ cup)

½ cup sour cream or Crème Fraiche *(page 39)*

½ cup grated jack, Swiss or other mild cheese

Preheat oven to 400°.

Cover the *tomatillos* with cold water. Bring to a boil and cook until soft, but not mushy. They will turn olive green when done. Drain the *tomatillos* and transfer them to a bowl. Mash them with a wooden spoon or potato masher. (If using canned *tomatillos*, just drain and mash them.)

In a large skillet, sauté the chiles and garlic in 2 tablespoons of oil. After 1 minute, add the *tomatillos*. Turn down the heat and simmer for 20 minutes, stirring frequently. Remove from heat and add the cilantro.

Combine the crab meat with enough sauce to moisten it, about ½ cup. Taste and adjust seasoning. Set aside.

In a small skillet, fry the tortillas in ¼ inch of oil until soft, about 30 seconds, and drain on paper towels.

Spoon a little sauce into the bottom of a baking dish big enough to hold the enchiladas in one layer. Divide the crab mixture into 8 portions. Spread one across the center of each tortilla. Roll the tortillas and place them, seams down, in the baking dish. Pour the remaining sauce over the enchiladas. Top each enchilada with a dollop of sour cream (thinned with a little milk if necessary). Sprinkle with cheese and bake for 10 minutes. Serve immediately.

Yellow Curried Crab

Thai curries come in three colors and three levels of spiciness. Red curries, made with dried red chiles, are the hottest. Green curries, prepared with fresh chiles, are in the middle and yellow curries are not hot at all.

Serves 6–8 as a side dish   Serves 4 as a main dish

3 tablespoons oil

1 medium yellow onion, chopped

1 teaspoon chopped ginger

1 tablespoon chopped garlic

3 tablespoons oil

1 teaspoon mild curry powder

1½ cups chicken stock

1 teaspoon fish sauce (page 40)

1 pound crab meat

2 red potatoes, peeled and cut into ½-inch dice

Sauté the onions, ginger and garlic in oil until the onions are soft. Add the curry powder and cook another minute. Add the stock and fish sauce. Bring to a boil, add the crab and potatoes, and simmer until the potatoes are cooked, about 6–8 minutes. Serve over rice.

Cioppino

Cioppino is said to have been created by San Francisco's fishing community using the local Dungeness crab and rockfish. Other fish and shellfish are often included in the tradition of all fisherman's stews. It can be prepared with blue crab or any other variety.

Serves 8

1 2½-pound live crab

1½ pounds tomatoes, peeled, seeded and chopped with skins, seeds and juice reserved or 1 large can Italian plum tomatoes, juice reserved

2 quarts Fumet (page 252)

8 clams

1 or more cups dry white wine

2 tablespoons chopped parsley

2 tablespoons or more chopped garlic

2 bay leaves

1 teaspoon fresh herbs such as thyme or oregano or ¼ teaspoon dried

16 mussels, debearded

1 pound rockfish filets (or any firm white fish)

Salt and pepper to taste

¼ cup Rouille (page 261)

Clean and crack the crab, reserving the shell. Add the tomato peels and seeds or juice and the crab shell to the *fumet*. Simmer 30 minutes and strain. Place the clams in a large, heavy pot or casserole. Add the *fumet* and, if necessary, white wine to cover the clams. Add the bay leaves, parsley, garlic, tomatoes and herbs. Cover and bring to a boil. Add the mussels and crab. Simmer 3–4 minutes until clams and mussels are open. Add the rockfish and cook 2–3 minutes more.

Serve immediately in heated soup bowls accompanied with hot French bread and *rouille*.

Braised Crab

Alternatives: *Lobster*   *Serves 4*

2 tablespoons butter

2 tablespoons olive oil

2 2-pound live crabs, cleaned
and cracked, fat reserved

2 tablespoons or more
chopped garlic

¼ cup chopped parsley

1 tablespoon fresh thyme

Black pepper to taste

1½ cups dry white wine

¼ cup Fumet (page 252)

2 tomatoes, peeled, seeded
and diced

In a wok or large skillet, heat the butter and olive oil. Add the crab and sauté over a high flame for 2 minutes. Add the garlic, herbs, wine, *fumet*, crab fat and pepper. Cover and cook at highest heat until shell is red, about 3 minutes. Remove the crab to a warm serving plate. Reduce the sauce at least by half over high heat. Toss the tomatoes in the sauce.

Arrange the crab legs on a heated serving platter or individual plates in a lifelike pattern. Pour the sauce over the crab, garnishing with the tomatoes.

Crab Gumbo

"Gumbo" encompasses a whole range of Louisiana recipes that are thickened with either okra or filé powder. Some include chicken or sausage as well as seafood. Our recipe is an all-seafood version based on crab stock, but feel free to improvise!

Serves 8

1 2½-pound live crab or 8 blue crabs	2 tablespoons or more chopped garlic
1 pound whole prawns or shrimp	½ teaspoon cayenne
3 pounds tomatoes, peeled, seeded and chopped, juice and skins reserved	2 bay leaves
	1 sprig fresh thyme or ½ teaspoon dried
2 tablespoons flour	Zest of 1 lemon
2–3 tablespoons butter	1 pound rockfish filet or any firm white fish
1 large bell pepper, diced	2 tablespoons filé powder
2 onions, diced	Salt and pepper to taste

In a large kettle or stockpot, steam or boil the crab, reserving the cooking liquid. Cool the crab quickly in ice water and drain thoroughly. Clean the crab, reserving the fat. Add the cleaned shell back to the pot, and set the crab aside. Shell the shrimp and add the shells and heads to the pot. Add the tomato skins, seeds and juice, bring to a boil, simmer for at least 30 minutes and strain.

In a pot big enough to hold all the ingredients, melt the butter and add enough flour to absorb the butter and form a thin paste. Cook this *roux* over gentle heat, stirring frequently, until it is a golden brown. Stir in the crab fat. Add the bell pepper, onion, garlic and cayenne and cook for a few minutes until the onion and pepper soften. Add the stock, herbs, lemon zest and tomatoes and simmer for 30 minutes.

Meanwhile, separate and crack the crab claws and legs, devein the shrimp if desired and cut the rockfish into bite-sized pieces. Add the fish and shellfish and the filé powder to the pot during the last 5 minutes or so. Do not boil after this point, or the filé powder will become bitter and stringy. Simmer until the fish and shrimp are just done and correct the seasoning.

Serve the gumbo in bowls over rice. Pass additional filé powder and Tabasco or another hot pepper sauce if desired.

(Note: This dish can be made with precooked crab as well. Simply start the stock with water or a mild *fumet* in place of the crab cooking liquid.)

Stir-Fried Crab

Alternatives: *Lobster*   *Serves 4 or more as a side dish*
Serves 2 as a main course

2 tablespoons salted black beans (page 42)

2 tablespoons sherry or rice wine

A 2–2½-pound live crab, cleaned, cut into serving pieces and cracked, fat reserved

Cornstarch

3 tablespoons oil

2 tablespoons chopped garlic

2 tablespoons chopped ginger

2 tablespoons soy sauce

2 teaspoons sugar

¼ cup water

4 scallions, trimmed into 1-inch lengths and then cut in half

1 teaspoon cornstarch dissolved in 1 tablespoon water

Cilantro for garnish

Coarsely chop the black beans and combine with the sherry. Let the mixture stand for 30 minutes.

Dip the cut ends of the crab legs and claws into cornstarch.

Heat the oil in a wok or heavy skillet. Stir-fry the garlic and ginger for 30 seconds; do not brown. Add the crab pieces and toss thoroughly. Add the soy sauce, sugar, water, scallions and reserved crab fat. Cook over high heat until the crab is done, 2–3 minutes. Add the cornstarch-water mixture, and cook until the sauce thickens. Garnish with cilantro and serve.

CRAYFISH
(Astacus pacifasticus)

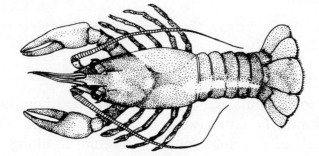

Other Names: *Crawfish, crawdad.*

Description: *Reddish brown when alive. Bright red when cooked.*

Size: *2–8 ounces.*

Range: *Rivers and estuaries of North America.*

Season: *Varies locally with water conditions. Generally spring-early fall in California.*

Fat Content: *Low (in meat).*

Yield: *15–20% meat.*

Available Forms: *Live, whole cooked.*

Similar Species: *Louisiana crayfish (Procambarus spp.) are generally flown in during the winter months.*

An important ingredient in Creole and Cajun cooking, these small freshwater crustaceans are found on every continent except Africa. They are highly regarded in Europe, but relatively unknown in much of North America. However, as lobster becomes prohibitively expensive, many Americans are discovering its delicious little cousin.

Crayfish are easily aquacultured. The current production is primarily in Louisiana, which exports thousands of tons of crayfish to Europe annually. Even California's small commercial harvest is largely exported.

Hot or cold, crayfish are best eaten with the fingers. Most of the meat is in the tail, but the delicious fat in the head should not be missed.

Crayfish Boil

This traditional Louisiana feast is ideally served outdoors. The crayfish should be eaten with the fingers so that the head, which is full of delicious fat, can be enjoyed along with the meaty tail. If you are eating indoors, cover the table and provide bowls for the shells.

Serves 4-6

1 gallon water

2 cups red wine

3 onions, chopped

3 scallions, chopped

½ cup chopped parsley

3 stalks celery, chopped

½ package shrimp boil spices (sold in most supermarkets)

Garlic to taste (at least 8 whole cloves)

Cayenne to taste (at least 1 teaspoon)

Salt and pepper to taste

2 pounds new potatoes, unpeeled

3 pounds live crayfish

Bring all the ingredients except for the crayfish and potatoes to a boil in a large pot. Simmer 30 minutes. Add the potatoes and cook 5 minutes. Add the crayfish and cook until done, about 8 minutes more.

Serve the crayfish and potatoes hot or chilled, accompanied with a spicy mayonnaise such as Creole Mayonnaise (page 258) or Aioli (page 259).

Crayfish Bisque

Serves 4 as a first course

1½ pounds live crayfish

1 bay leaf

½ cup diced celery

1 cup diced onion

¼ cup butter

Pinch cayenne

1 tablespoon fresh thyme

3 cups milk and 1 cup cream
or 2 cups milk and 2 cups
half-and-half

Salt and white pepper to taste

Chopped chives for garnish

Boil the crayfish in water for about 7–8 minutes with the bay leaf and half the vegetables. Cool and reserve ½ cup of the cooking liquid. Shell and devein the crayfish, reserving the fat and shells. Chop the meat finely, combine it with the fat and set aside.

Chop the heads and shells with a knife or food processor. Heat the butter and cayenne in a large saucepan. Sauté the remaining vegetables gently until soft. Add the shells and debris, thyme and reserved liquid. Simmer 15–20 minutes. Strain the liquid into a smaller saucepan. Add the milk and cream, bring to a simmer and add the crayfish meat and fat. Remove from heat, season with salt and pepper, and ladle into individual serving bowls. Garnish with chopped chives.

EEL

(Anguilla anguilla)

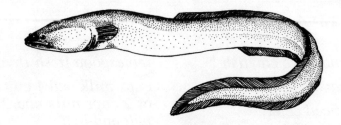

Description: *Dark green to black, fading to yellow.*	**Fat Content:** *High.*
Size: *To 3 feet.*	**Season:** *Sporadically available all year.*
Range: *Coastal and inland waters of the northern Atlantic coast.*	**Available forms:** *Live, dressed, smoked.*
Yield: *About 70% meat.*	

Eel is a favorite food in Europe, but is generally ignored by Americans. In their natural habitat, eel breed in salt water and live either in shallow coastal waters or in fresh water. In many countries, eel is aquacultured in fresh water. Unfortunately, they are expensive to raise because eel will eat only fish protein.

Eel can be stewed or grilled with excellent results. Teriyaki Sauce (page 264) makes a wonderful marinade.

To Skin an Eel

Like catfish, eel has tough skin which should be removed before the meat is cooked. See directions for skinning a catfish (page 82).

Eel Stewed in Red Wine

Serves 3–4

2 tablespoons olive oil

1 yellow onion, chopped

1–2 tablespoons chopped
garlic

1 pound eel, cleaned and cut
into 2-inch lengths

1 cup canned tomatoes with
juice, chopped

2 cups red wine

2 cups Fumet (page 252)

1 ounce pine nuts

1 tablespoon chopped parsley

1 tablespoon vinegar

Salt and pepper to taste

Sauté the onion and garlic in oil in a casserole or heavy saucepan large enough to hold all the ingredients. When the onions
are translucent, add the eel and toss the pieces in the oil. Add
the remaining ingredients. Cover and simmer slowly for 30
minutes. Serve over rice or with French bread.

FLOUNDER

Starry Flounder
(Platichthys stellatus)

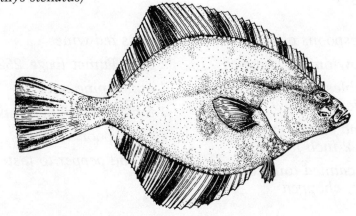

Description: *Dark brown to black with rough skin above. Creamy to white below. Orange-white and black stripes on fins.*	**Season:** *All year, especially winter months.*
Size: *1–6 pounds. Smaller fish are milder in flavor.*	**Fat Content:** *Low.*
	Yield: *40% filet.*
Range: *Central California to Alaska.*	**Available Forms:** *Round, filet.*

Winter Flounder
(Pseudopleuronectes americanus)

Other Names: *Lemon sole (smaller fish only).*	**Season:** *Fall to spring.*
Description: *Rust-brown mottled with black above.*	**Fat Content:** *Low.*
Size: *1–2 pounds. Occasionally to 5 pounds.*	**Yield:** *40% filet.*
Range: *Atlantic coast. Chesapeake Bay to southern Canada.*	**Available Forms:** *Filet, round.*

Summer Flounder

(Paralichthys dentatus)

Other Names: *Fluke.*	**Season:** *Summer.*
Description: *Mottled grey-brown to olive-green above.*	**Fat Content:** *Low.*
Size: *2–5 pounds and up.*	**Yield:** *50% filet.*
Range: *Atlantic. Carolinas to New England.*	**Available Forms:** *Round, filet, steak.*

Perhaps no fish is a better example of the maxim "familiarity breeds contempt." Because of the wide availability of flounder, it seems mundane to most restaurants and their patrons. However, with its delicate but distinctive flavor and agreeable texture, starry flounder is certainly in a league with the more popular Pacific flatfish. Flounder filets can be freely substituted in any sole recipe. Pan-dressed flounder may be grilled or baked, with the skin adding a characteristic flavor. Filets with the skin attached are tricky to grill as they tend to curl. Skinless filets are suitable for sautéing, poaching and, if on the large side, broiling. Choose a delicate sauce such as Beurre Blanc (page 253) or a cream-based sauce.

Alternatives: *Petrale or other soles.*

Broiled Flounder Filets with Herb Butter

Some appropriate fresh herbs are suggested below. One or two
is plenty; too many herbs become confusing. Pungent herbs
such as rosemary, oregano or tarragon are not suitable for the
delicate taste of flounder.

Serves 4

4 tablespoons softened butter

*2 tablespoons chopped fresh
herbs such as parsley,
thyme, watercress, chervil,
chives or basil*

Salt and pepper to taste

Juice of ½ lemon

1–1½ pounds flounder filets

Preheat the broiler.

Blend the butter, herbs, salt, pepper and lemon juice. Arrange
the filets skin side down on a buttered roasting pan. Spread the
herb butter on top of the filets and broil close to the heat until
just done.

Transfer the filets to warm plates and drizzle with any butter
remaining in the pan.

Flounder Baked with Fresh Herbs

This is one of the simplest and least caloric ways to use flounder, and also a delicious one. Herbs suggested on page 122 are also appropriate here.

Serves 4

1–1½ pounds flounder filets   *1–2 tablespoons chopped*
Salt and pepper to taste   *fresh herbs*
Juice of ½ lemon

Preheat oven to 500°.

Season the fish with salt, pepper and lemon juice. Spread with a generous layer of chopped herbs. Place filets skin side down on a flameproof platter or shallow baking dish. Cover tightly with foil. Bake until just done by the skewer test, about 5–8 minutes. Serve with lemon wedges.

Grilled Herb-Stuffed Flounder in Grape Leaves

Once again, flounder and fresh herbs are combined. In this recipe, however, these delicate flavors are a foil to the more aromatic grape leaves and charcoal-grilled flavor. This dish was originally conceived as a main dish, with whole filets stuffed and wrapped in lettuce or other large leaves. But the flounder that day turned out to be very small, we had grape leaves on hand and somehow the idea of fish *dolmas* came to mind. This dish may be made in advance as an appetizer to an outdoor barbecue.

Serves 8 as an appetizer

2–3 cloves garlic	*Juice of 1 lemon*
¼ cup chopped fresh herbs such as parsley, basil, thyme or chives	*1½–2 pounds flounder filets*
	24 bottled grape leaves, drained, stems trimmed

Press the garlic into a small bowl, add the herbs and lemon juice and combine.

Divide the filets into 1-ounce pieces, roughly rectangular. (If some of the filets are large, the thick end can be sliced in half horizontally.)

Flatten the grape leaves, dull side up and stem end toward you on the board. Place a piece of filet spread with the herb mixture on each leaf and roll it into a cylinder. Starting with the base of the leaf, wrap the leaf around the rolled filet, tucking in the sides of the leaf like the flaps of an envelope. The roll should be a tight bundle with only the point of the leaf opposite the stem showing. Chill the rolls until ready to grill. (These can be assembled several hours ahead of time.)

Oil the rolls lightly and grill until the leaves are well marked but not burnt. Serve on platters to be eaten with the fingers.

GROUPER

(Family Serranidae)

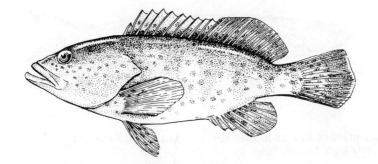

Other Names: *Sea bass, various species names.*	**Range:** *Worldwide in tropical and temperate waters.*
Description: *Deep-bodied with projecting mandibles. Color varies according to species.*	**Season:** *Sporadically all year.*
	Fat Content: *Low.*
	Yield: *30–40% filet, depending on size.*
Size: *Smaller species in 2–3-pound range. Larger species to several hundred pounds.*	**Available Forms:** *Round, filet, steak.*

This large cosmopolitan family includes many important food fishes. Although some are found off the Pacific coast, most grouper are flown in from the eastern United States or New Zealand. All species are likely to be marketed as grouper or sea-bass. The relatively rare giant seabass *(Stereolepis gigas)* of the Pacific coast, while unrelated, is also marketed as grouper.

The firm, lean flesh of the grouper falls somewhere between' halibut and the basses in flavor and texture, and is suitable to the same cooking methods as these varieties. Smaller filets and tail portions are easily grilled or broiled; larger sections may be cut into steaks or diagonal slices up to an inch thick for the same treatments, or may be stuffed and baked with Oyster Stuffing for Fish (page 166). Grouper is also a good choice for soups and stews.

GRUNION

(Leuresthes tenius)

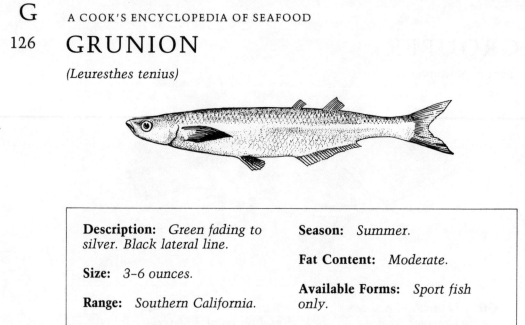

Description: *Green fading to silver. Black lateral line.*	**Season:** *Summer.*
Size: *3–6 ounces.*	**Fat Content:** *Moderate.*
Range: *Southern California.*	**Available Forms:** *Sport fish only.*

The grunion is a small member of the smelt family which spawns above high tide in the light of the full moon. A sport fish, it can only legally be taken by hand; no nets or other equipment are allowed.

Grunion may be cooked in the same manner as jacksmelt or whitebait although it should be boned if eaten whole.

HALIBUT

Pacific Halibut

(Hippoglossus stenolepis)

Description: *Greenish brown above.*	**Season:** *Highly regulated and local. Primarily winter.*
Size: *10–100 pounds and up.*	**Fat Content:** *Low.*
Range: *Pacific Ocean from southern California north.*	**Yield:** *Up to 65% filet.*
	Available Forms: *Pan-dressed, steak, filet, fletch (half filet).*

California Halibut

(Paralichthys californicus)

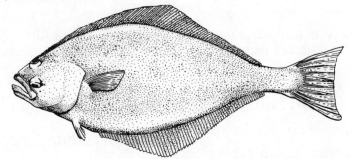

Description: *Olive green to black above. White or variegated below. Right-eyed nearly as often as left-eyed.*	**Season:** *All year.*
	Fat Content: *Low.*
Size: *5–35 pounds.*	**Yield:** *65% filet.*
Range: *Baja to central California.*	**Available Forms:** *Round, filet, fletch, occasionally steak.*

Of the two local halibut species, the larger Pacific variety is slightly preferable and considerably scarcer. Both are excellent if not overcooked. The dense, mild and slightly sweet flesh of halibut is excellent for grilling, broiling and sautéing. Serve with a compound butter (pages 254–55), Fresh Tomato Salsa (page 262) or Green Chile Sauce (page 264).

Alternatives: *Greenland halibut (A), grouper (A,G,P).*

Sautéed Halibut with Cream and Herbs

Alternatives: *Snapper, grouper (A,G,P), sole, flounder (A,P)*   *Serves 4*
fancy rockfish

1–1½ pounds halibut filet

2 tablespoons butter

1 teaspoon chopped shallots

1 teaspoon lemon zest

*1 tablespoon chopped fresh
herbs such as parsley,
chervil, chives, thyme,
tarragon or dill*

*1 cup Crème Fraîche
(page 39) or whipping
cream*

Salt and white pepper to taste

Cut the halibut into serving pieces. Thin tail filets may be cut straight across; filets over an inch thick are best cut diagonally into slices or scallops.

Melt half the butter in a skillet large enough to hold all the pieces. Sauté the fish gently until just short of done and transfer to hot plates or a serving dish. (The fish will finish cooking on its own.) If the butter in the pan has browned, discard it.

Add the remaining butter to the pan with the shallots and lemon zest. Cook without browning for a minute or so. Add the herbs and *crème fraiche* and a pinch of salt and pepper. Bring to a boil, reduce by half and correct the seasoning.

If the fish has cooled noticeably, return it to the pan briefly to reheat. Otherwise, pour the sauce over the fish and serve, accompanied by a colorful assortment of steamed vegetables.

Variations

This technique can be used for a wide variety of fish (see above for alternatives). It also lends itself to many sauce variations:

Use ginger and lime or orange zest in place of the shallots and herbs; garnish with julienned scallions.

A scant teaspoon of tomato paste or a tablespoon of fresh tomato sauce will produce a pale pink *sauce aurore*. Omit the lemon zest and stick to the milder herbs in this case.

Soak a few saffron threads or a pinch of powdered saffron in the cream for an hour or so, and omit the herbs.

Add 2 tablespoons mashed or puréed avocado to the cream sauce just before serving in place of the herbs and lemon zest. Heat but do not cook or the avocado will become bitter. Garnish with lime zest.

Salt-Grilled Halibut

Salting fish before grilling is a typically Japanese technique, used to draw out any strong flavors. Any fish suitable for grilling may be salt-grilled. Milder fish such as halibut are salted the least, while stronger fish such as salmon or mackerel are more heavily salted.

Serves 4

1–1½ pounds halibut steaks or filets	*Sliced raw vegetables such as carrots and cucumbers for garnish*
Salt	

Dipping Sauce

4 tablespoons soy sauce	*2 tablespoons lemon juice or rice vinegar*

Cover the steaks on both sides with a thin layer of salt. Refrigerate for one hour. Combine the soy sauce and lemon juice. Set aside.

Grill the steaks until done by the skewer test. Serve the fish with the dipping sauce, garnished with slices of raw vegetables.

Steamed Halibut in Nori Seaweed

Nori, a Japanese seaweed which is shredded and dried in sheets, is best known as the wrapping for rolled *sushi*. It also makes a delicious wrapping for steamed fish, imparting a characteristic flavor and aroma to mild fish. *Nori*, which is extremely nutritious, is available in Asian markets.

Alternatives: *Grouper (A,G,P), snapper (G),   Serves 4
the basses (A,G,P), fancy rockfish*

1–1½ pounds halibut filet

*1 teaspoon wasabi powder
(page 44)*

Water

4 sheets nori (8–10 inches square)

Dipping sauce for Salt-Grilled Halibut (page 129)

Choose a thick piece of halibut if possible; an inch or so is ideal. Blend the *wasabi* with enough water to form a smooth paste. Slice the filet crosswise into serving pieces. Fold the thin pieces cut from the tail in half to form a thicker portion. Spread one side of each piece with a small amount of the *wasabi* paste.

Sprinkle a sheet of *nori* with just enough water to make it pliable. Place a piece of fish, bone side down, diagonally across the middle of the sheet. Fold the sheet around the fish, forming an envelope. Repeat for the other pieces of fish. Steam the packages on a plate, about 8 minutes per inch of thickness. Serve with rice and the dipping sauce.

PACIFIC HERRING

(Clupea harengus pallasii)

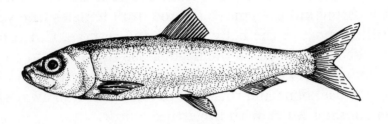

Description: *Silvery blue-green fading to white. Loose scales.*	**Season:** *Late fall–early winter, while spawning.*
Size: *2–4 per pound.*	**Fat Content:** *High.*
	Yield: *50% filet.*
Range: *Pacific coast. Northern Baja California north.*	**Available Forms:** *Round, pickled, salted, smoked.*

San Francisco Bay is a major spawning ground for the Pacific herring. Most of the catch is sent to Japan where the roe is a high-priced delicacy, making the brief herring season a lucrative one for the Northern California fishermen. A small amount of the catch stays here and is available locally.

Herring's moderate to pronounced flavor and soft texture make it ideal for pickling, but it may also be cooked when fresh.

Herring, like other rich fish, takes well to grilling. A preliminary marinade of olive oil, salt, pepper and herbs complements the charcoal flavor nicely. Fresh or dried thyme, rosemary, oregano or marjoram are good choices for herbs. Allow ¾–1 pound of whole fish per person.

Whole herring roes may be cured in brine according to the general procedure for Caviar (page 232); use a 15% salt solution and omit cutting open the egg sac.

To Clean and Bone Herring

To clean herring, make a slit from the vent to below the jaw with a paring knife. Remove the roe from females (the yellow sac filling most of the belly cavity) and reserve. Cut through the backbone just behind the head, grasp the head and pull the head and entrails away from the body. Remove the dark strip along the backbone and rinse the cavity well. Rub away scales under running water with fingertips.

To bone a herring, especially if you are going to stuff or grill it, place the fish belly side down on the board. Press down from the top, forcing the two filets apart. Turn the fish over and peel the backbone away from the filets, leaving them attached to the skin and tail.

Baked Herring with Tomatoes and White Wine

Serves 4

2 tablespoons olive oil

2 tablespoons chopped garlic

½ yellow onion, julienned

1 pound tomatoes, peeled, seeded and chopped or 2 cups canned peeled tomatoes, drained and chopped

½ teaspoon fresh (or ¼ teaspoon dried) oregano, thyme or marjoram

2½–3 pounds herring, round

¼ cup white wine

Salt and pepper to taste

Sauté the garlic and onion in oil until soft but not browned. Add the tomatoes and herbs and cook until most of the liquid is evaporated. Season to taste.

Clean the herring, leaving the backbones in. Place them in a single layer in a baking dish. Add the wine and the tomato sauce, cover, and bake 12–15 minutes or until filets pull away from bones easily. Remove the fish to a warm serving dish;

reduce the sauce if it is too watery, and pour over the fish. Serve with plain or saffron-flavored rice.

Grilled Stuffed Herring Brochettes

Alternatives: *Anchovies, whitebait*   *Serves 4*

2 pounds herring, cleaned and boned

Olive oil

Lemon wedges for garnish

Bread Crumb Stuffing

3 tablespoons olive oil

¼ cup chopped garlic

¼ cup chopped parsley

¼ cup bread crumbs

¼ cup Parmesan or Romano cheese, grated

Salt and pepper to taste

Sauté garlic in oil until cooked but not browned. Add other stuffing ingredients, and combine. Season to taste with salt and pepper.

Place the filets on a cutting board, skin side down. Spread each filet with a layer of the stuffing and roll toward the tail. Skewer several together, brush with a little olive oil and grill over a hot fire on both sides until filets are cooked through. Serve with lemon wedges.

Pickled Herring

For 5 pounds of herring

Preliminary curing:

2 quarts water	*10 ounces salt (coarse or*
1 quart vinegar	*Kosher salt is preferable)*

Filet or pan-dress the fish. Place in a stainless steel or glass bowl. Combine the water, vinegar and salt and cover the fish, reserving any excess for the final pickling. Refrigerate for 48 hours, drain and cover with fresh water. Soak for several hours to remove excess salt, drain and proceed with the final pickling.

Sweet and Sour Pickle

1 small red onion, thinly sliced	*Water and vinegar*
1 carrot, thinly sliced	*Salt and sugar to taste*
2 tablespoons commercial pickling spice mixture	

Arrange the cured fish in layers alternately with the onion, carrot and spices. Cover with a mixture of 2 parts vinegar to 1 part water, adding salt and sugar to taste. Refrigerate for another 24 hours or more before serving.

Sour Cream Pickle

Cover with half sour cream and half vinegar-water mixture (2 parts vinegar, 1 part water) and omit the sugar. Add a little Dijon mustard, if desired.

Herring Roe Sautéed with Bacon

Try this variation on the theme of "bacon and eggs" as an appetizer in a meal featuring grilled or baked herring.

Serves 8 as an appetizer

1 pound herring roe	*Lemon wedges for garnish*
2 slices bacon, diced	

Herring roe is available during herring season at many fish markets.

Discard any roe sacs that are badly damaged, as they will disintegrate in cooking. Soak the intact roe sacs in salted water for at least 30 minutes and drain.

Sauté the bacon in a large skillet until crisp. Remove bacon, pour off all but 2 tablespoons of fat, and sauté the roe over moderate heat until it just turns opaque. Squeeze some lemon juice over the roe in the pan, and serve with the bacon and additional lemon wedges.

JACK MACKEREL

(Trachurus symmetricus)

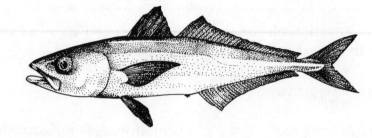

Other Names: *Spanish mackerel, Pacific jack.*	**Season:** *All year. Less common in summer.*
Description: *Metallic blue to olive green above. Silver below.*	**Fat Content:** *High.*
	Yield: *50% filet.*
Size: *To 1 pound.*	**Available Forms:** *Round.*
Range: *Pacific coast. Mainly central Mexico to southern California.*	

In taxonomic terms, this is a jack and not a mackerel, but in culinary terms it is interchangeable with the mackerels and bonito.

JACKSMELT

(Atherinopsis californiensis)

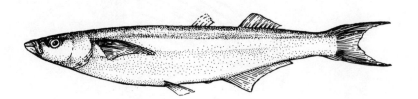

Description: *Greenish blue fading to silver. Prominent light blue lateral line.*	Range: *California coast.*
	Fat Content: *Moderate.*
Size: *½–1½ pounds.*	Yield: *80% pan-dressed.*
Season: *Winter and spring.*	Available Forms: *Round.*

Jacksmelt is an underrated and underutilized fish. It has mild, fairly firm flesh which pulls away easily from its large bones. Jacksmelt can be marinated in olive oil and herbs and then grilled, baked in sauce, braised as in Braised Mackerel with Tomatoes, Rosemary and Garlic (page 145) or breaded and pan-fried.

JOHN DORY

(Zenopsis spp.)

Other Names: *St. Pierre.*	**Fat Content:** *Moderate.*
Description: *Pale silver. Black dot surrounded by a yellow halo.*	**Yield:** *25% filet.*
	Available Forms: *Filet.*
Size: *3-6 pounds common.*	
Range: *Northern Atlantic. Mediterranean. Western Pacific continental slopes.*	

This vertically compressed fish is occasionally available on the West Coast in filet form, and has excellent cooking qualities. Its fine flavor and texture make it suitable for sole recipes.

LINGCOD
(Ophiodon elongatus)

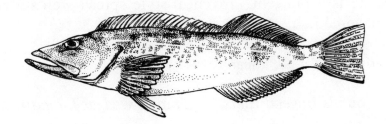

Description: *Variable. Brownish green to vivid blue-green. Dark spots or mottling.*	**Fat Content:** *Low.*
Size: *3 pounds and up.*	**Yield:** *40% filet.*
Range: *Baja California to Alaska.*	**Available Forms:** *Round, filet, steak, smoked.*
Season: *All year. Primarily winter.*	

While not a true cod, lingcod is one of the more important food fishes on the West Coast. Several species of the unrelated but similar greenlings (*Hexagrammos* spp.) are also marketed as lingcod, and are interchangeable in cooking characteristics. The lings vary in more than skin color; the flesh of some individuals, especially juveniles, is a bright blue-green although this color disappears with cooking.

The relatively dense flesh of lingcod takes a surprisingly long time to cook. Thinner tail filets are easily grilled or broiled, but thicker pieces are better suited to slower, moist-heat methods. Smaller filets may be used interchangeably with rockfish or cabezon.

Alternatives: *Cod (A,P).*

Baked Lingcod with Tapenade

Tapenade is a pungent Provençal-style spread well suited to mild-flavored fish.

Alternatives: *Angler (A), firmer rockfish*   *Serves 4*

1–1½ pounds lingcod filets   *Lemon wedges for garnish*

Tapenade

*4 canned anchovy filets,
rinsed and chopped*

3 or 4 cloves garlic, peeled

*½ cup Niçoise or other black
olives, pitted and roughly
chopped*

1 tablespoon capers

1 teaspoon lemon zest

Black pepper to taste

Preheat oven to 500°.

In a mortar and pestle or blender, mix the anchovies and garlic to a paste, add the olives, capers and lemon zest; blend until smooth, adding a bit of olive oil if necessary. Add black pepper to taste.

Place the lingcod filets skin side down on a piece of aluminum foil large enough to completely enclose them. Spread the top with the *tapenade* and fold over the foil, sealing around the edge. Bake on a sheet pan for 8–12 minutes, or until a skewer poked through the foil easily penetrates the thickest part of the filets. Place the package on a warm platter and slit open the side opposite the seal; the filets can then be slid out of the package complete with the cooking juices. Serve with lemon wedges.

Individual Serving Method

Cut the filet into individual slices or scallops. Place each on a rectangle of parchment or baking paper (available in cookware shops), spread with the *tapenade* and seal the packages. Bake 6–8 minutes. Serve the fish in its packages, allowing each diner to open his own to release its wonderful aroma.

Indonesian Curried Lingcod

This recipe comes from a delightful book, *Indonesian Food and Cookery* by Sri Owen (Prospect Books, London). Indonesian fish curries often combine coconut milk with aromatic spices such as turmeric and coriander, producing more delicate flavors than Indian curries.

Alternatives: *Sculpin, rockfish, sablefish, catfish*　　　*Serves 4 as a main course*

2 tablespoons oil

1 tablespoon chopped garlic

4 shallots or 1 large yellow onion, chopped

1 tablespoon chopped ginger

½ tablespoon dried or 1 blade fresh lemongrass, chopped

1 teaspoon chile powder

1–2 teaspoons ground coriander

1 teaspoon turmeric

1 tablespoon tamarind paste (page 43) dissolved in 3 tablespoons cold water

1 cup coconut milk (page 39)

1 pound lingcod filets, cut into 1-inch cubes

Mint or cilantro for garnish

Sauté the garlic, shallots and ginger in oil, in a wok or large skillet, until the shallots are translucent. Add lemongrass, chile powder, coriander and turmeric, and sauté the mixture for 2 minutes. Add the tamarind water and coconut milk. Simmer slowly for 2–3 minutes. Add the fish filets. Cook until the fish is done. Garnish with mint or cilantro. Serve over rice.

This dish may be accompanied by Fresh Cilantro Chutney (page 265).

LOBSTER

American Lobster

(Homarus americanus)

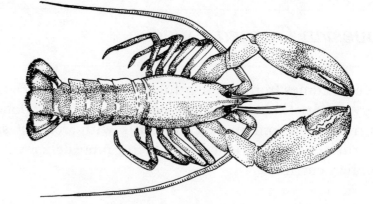

Other Names: *Maine lobster.*	**Season:** *All year.*
Description: *Orange-red to blue-green with dark mottling. Bright red when cooked.*	**Fat Content:** *Low.*
Size: *1–5 pounds.*	**Yield:** *25% meat.*
Range: *New England to southern Canada.*	**Available Forms:** *Live, picked meat.*

Lobster is the most prized American seafood and one of the most expensive. Due to overfishing, populations have diminished noticeably. Unless current trends are altered (which seems unlikely) or there is a breakthrough in lobster aquaculture, supplies will continue to decrease and prices continue to rise.

The roe of female lobsters, called "coral," is prized as an ingredient in sauces. "Tomalley," the liver and surrounding fat, is found in both sexes and is also delicious.

Traditionally, lobster is boiled, steamed or grilled and served with a range of sauces, often quite rich. It can be made into a deliciously rich soup or bisque such as Crayfish Bisque (page 117) or served cold with various mayonnaises (pages 257–59).

The Chinese stir-fry pieces of lobster tail in black bean sauce, as in Stir-Fried Crab (page 114).

Spiny Lobster

(Panulirus spp.*)*

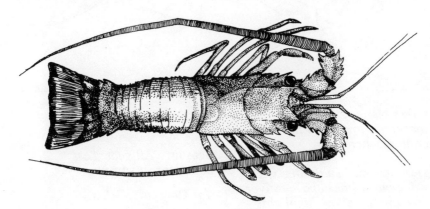

Other Names: *Rock lobster, crayfish, langouste.*	**Season:** *All year.*
Description: *Similar to the American lobster but with brighter mottling and no claws. Bright red when cooked.*	**Fat Content:** *Low (in meat).*
	Yield: *25% meat.*
Size: *1–4 pounds.*	**Available Forms:** *Live.*
Range: *Warm coastal waters of the world.*	

Spiny lobster makes up the bulk of the frozen lobster market. Many are imported from South Africa and the far Pacific. Lobster tails are usually split and grilled or broiled. They can be boiled in a flavored stock such as Crayfish Boil (page 116). Use in recipes for crayfish or lobster.

PACIFIC MACKEREL

(Scomber japonicus)

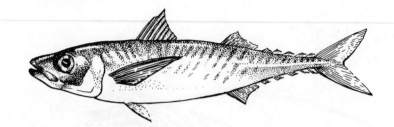

Other Names: *Boston mackerel, American mackerel, chub mackerel.*	**Range:** *Throughout the Pacific.*
	Season: *All year. Less abundant in summer.*
Description: *Dark blue with wavy black lines above. Silvery green with yellow highlights below.*	**Fat Content:** *High.*
	Yield: *50% filet.*
Size: *To 2 pounds.*	**Available Forms:** *Round.*

The ubiquitous mackerels are perhaps our most undervalued family of fish. They have had more bad press down through the years than any other variety, primarily from people who don't like garlic, anchovies, olive oil or other Mediterranean flavors. When truly fresh and prepared with other robust-flavored ingre-dients, mackerel can be delicious. Of all fish, however, it demands freshness; everything that has been said about old mackerel is true.

Grilling and braising are appropriate cooking methods. Mackerel may also be poached and used in salads, or used in Sashimi (page 245), or Ceviche (page 70). Boned mackerel may be baked in foil with a bread crumb stuffing as in Grilled Stuffed Herring Brochettes (page 133) or Sicilian-Style Stuffing (page 57).

Alternatives: *Any species of Atlantic or Pacific mackerel, jack mackerel, bonito.*

Braised Mackerel with Tomatoes, Rosemary and Garlic

Alternatives: *Jacksmelt, tuna, bonito*   *Serves 4*

4 whole mackerel, approximately ½ pound each

2 tablespoons olive oil

½ pound tomatoes, peeled, seeded and chopped

2 teaspoons chopped garlic

1 teaspoon fresh rosemary or ½ teaspoon dried

¼ cup white wine

Dress the mackerel, leaving the heads on or discarding them as desired. In a skillet with a tight-fitting lid, heat the oil over moderate heat. Add the fish and cook briefly on each side, just until the flesh begins to stiffen. Add the remaining ingredients, cover, and cook until the fish is thoroughly cooked, about 7–10 minutes. Remove the fish, season the sauce to taste, reduce if necessary, and serve over the fish.

Steamed Mackerel with Daikon and Wasabi

Alternatives: *Bonito, tuna, any moderate-to-rich fish*   *Serves 4*

2 cups grated and peeled
  daikon (Japanese white
  radish, available at Asian
  groceries)

1–1½ pounds mackerel filet,
  skin on

Soy sauce

1 teaspoon wasabi powder
  (page 44)

Squeeze the excess moisture from the *daikon* and drain in a sieve or colander. Cut the fish into serving pieces and marinate in the soy sauce.

Sprinkle the *wasabi* over the *daikon* and combine. Spread this mixture on a plate. Arrange the fish pieces on top of the mixture and steam until the fish is done by the skewer test.

Serve the fish on a bed of *daikon*. If a sauce is desired, make a dipping sauce of a little more *wasabi* dissolved in soy sauce.

Grilled Mackerel with Egg Glaze

Alternatives: *Yellowtail, mahi-mahi, wahoo*   *Serves 4*

2 egg yolks

1 teaspoon sherry

1 teaspoon soy sauce

½ teaspoon sugar

1–1½ pounds mackerel filets,
  skin on

Combine the egg yolks, sherry, soy sauce and sugar. Dip the filets in the egg mixture and grill 2–3 minutes on a side, or until done, basting with the egg mixture. Serve as is or with a dipping sauce made from soy sauce and lemon juice.

MAHI-MAHI

(Coryphaena hippurus)

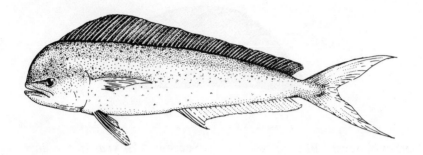

Other Names: *Dolphin, dolphinfish, dorado.*

Description: *Bright blue and green above. Yellow with blue spots below. Yellow tail.*

Size: *13–35 pounds.*

Range: *Warm oceans of the world.*

Season: *Spring–summer, sporadically all year.*

Fat Content: *Moderate.*

Yield: *25% filet.*

Available Forms: *Filet, steak.*

While this fish is properly called a dolphin, in order to avoid confusion with the mammal of the same name the Hawaiian name of mahi-mahi is becoming more widespread. A popular and beautiful game species, it is also available commercially, primarily from the waters of the far Pacific. However, the annual catch is quite small, and considerably more fish are sold than are actually caught; yellowtail and other jacks often make up the difference.

This firm, flavorful fish is best simply grilled or broiled. It really needs no sauce, just a squeeze of lemon or lime.

Alternatives: *Wahoo (A,P).*

MUSSEL

(Mytilus edulis and M. californianus)

Other Names: *Blue or bay mussel.*	**Season:** *All year in the East. November-April in the West.*
Description: *Bivalve. Dark blue to black. Smooth shell.*	**Fat Content:** *Low.*
Size: *12 per pound average.*	**Yield:** *40–50% edible portion.*
Range: *Atlantic coast from central United States to southern Canada. Pacific coast bays.*	**Available Forms:** *Live, shucked in the East, smoked.*

Highly regarded in Europe and generally neglected in this country, mussels are abundant and delicious. They are widely and successfully aquacultured in Europe, and are beginning to be produced in quantity in New England. Mussel culture on both coasts will probably become much more extensive in the near future.

Neither *M. edulis* nor the indigenous California mussel, *M. californianus*, has been widely harvested commercially on the Pacific coast, but they can be easily gathered from rocks at low tide. The California variety grows quite large; only mussels under 3 inches are tender. Both species are quarantined on the Pacific coast during the summer (page 281).

Mussels are generally steamed open when recipes call for shucked mussels; they may also be cooked in the shell. Substitute mussels in recipes for cooked clams or oysters.

To Clean and Debeard Mussels

To clean mussels, first grasp the "beard" (the bundle of fibers protruding from between the shells) and remove it with a quick tug. Check to see that the mussel is alive by twisting the shells against each other along the seam; shells of a live mussel will not slide easily. Discard any open mussels which do not close when handled. Scrub the shells well with a brush or a synthetic scrub pad, and rinse with fresh water. (Note: Mussels will not live as long after cleaning as they will unmolested, so avoid cleaning them before the day when they will be cooked.)

Fried Mussels with Tarator Sauce

Alternatives: *½ pound shucked oysters*   *Serves 4 as an appetizer*

1½ pounds mussels, cleaned and debearded

All-purpose flour

1 egg, beaten

½ cup fine bread crumbs

Oil for frying

1 recipe Tarator Sauce (page 262)

Steam open and shuck mussels (or shuck them raw); drain well. Dip mussels first in flour, then egg, then roll in bread crumbs. (Mussels may be prepared up to this point several hours in advance and refrigerated.) Fry at 375°. Drain on paper towels. Serve with Tarator Sauce.

Spinach Salad with Mussels and Cream

When mussels are in season, chef and teacher Jeremiah Tower serves them in many imaginative ways at the Santa Fe Bar & Grill in Berkeley and the Balboa Café in San Francisco. This is one of them.

Serves 2

½ pound mussels, cleaned and debearded

¼ cup white wine

¼ cup cream or Crème Fraîche (page 39)

½ pound fresh spinach leaves, washed, with stems removed

Juice of ½ lemon

Salt and pepper to taste

Steam the mussels open. Shuck them, reserving about 1 tablespoon of the juices, and chill. When cold, add the cream to the mussels and soak for several hours or overnight, refrigerated.

Dry the spinach well, taking care not to bruise the leaves. Toss them in a salad bowl with the lemon juice, salt and pepper until evenly moistened. Add the mussels and cream and toss until all the leaves are well coated.

Arrange on chilled plates, largest leaves on the bottom, with mussels in a circle on top.

Warm Spinach Salad with Mussels, Ginger and Garlic

Serves 2

½ pound fresh spinach
  leaves, washed, with
  stems removed

1 tablespoon lemon juice

Salt and pepper to taste

¾ pound mussels, cleaned
  and debearded

3 tablespoons olive oil

1 teaspoon chopped ginger

1 teaspoon chopped garlic

Dry the spinach leaves and toss them in a salad bowl with the lemon juice, salt and pepper until evenly moistened.

Steam and shuck the mussels. Heat the oil in a skillet; add the mussels, ginger and garlic and sauté gently, but do not brown. Pour the oil over the spinach and toss immediately, until the leaves are wilted but not cooked. Serve on warm plates.

Broiled Stuffed Mussels

Serves 4 as an appetizer

1 pound mussels, cleaned
  and debearded

¼ cup dry white wine

¼ cup bread crumbs

¼ cup grated Parmesan
  cheese

1 tablespoon chopped garlic

1 tablespoon melted butter

1 tablespoon chopped parsley

½ teaspoon black pepper

Lemon wedges for garnish

Preheat the broiler. Steam the mussels open in white wine in a heavy saucepan. Shuck the mussels and return them to half-shells. Combine the remaining ingredients and pack this mixture loosely into the shells on top of the mussels. Broil until the stuffing begins to brown, about 3–5 minutes. Serve with lemon wedges and pass Tabasco or another hot pepper sauce if desired.

Steamed Mussels with White Wine and Shallots

Moules Marinière

Serves 4 as an appetizer   Serves 2 as a main course

2 pounds mussels, cleaned
   and debearded

1 tablespoon chopped shallots

1 tablespoon chopped parsley

¼ cup dry white wine

Black pepper to taste

Combine all the ingredients in a heavy saucepan with a tight lid and bring to a boil. Steam the mussels until open, about 3–5 minutes. Serve in soup bowls with the liquid along with plenty of French bread to soak up the broth.

Steamed Mussels with Tomato, Garlic and White Wine

Serves 4 as an appetizer   Serves 2 as a main course

1 tablespoon olive oil

1 tablespoon chopped garlic

1 tablespoon chopped shallots

½ pound tomatoes, peeled,
   seeded and chopped or
   ½ small can tomatoes,
   chopped

2 pounds mussels, cleaned
   and debearded

1 tablespoon fresh herbs—
   parsley, thyme, basil

¼ cup dry white wine

Black pepper

Rouille (page 261)

In a heavy saucepan large enough to hold the mussels, sauté garlic, shallots and tomatoes in oil until soft. Add mussels, herbs, wine and pepper. Steam until mussels open, 3–5 minutes.

Serve as a soup with French bread and a garlicky mayonnaise such as *rouille*.

Rice Pilaf with Mussels

Serves 3-4

1 tablespoon oil

1 tablespoon chopped garlic

1 tablespoon chopped shallots

1 teaspoon paprika

1 cup white rice

*2 cups chicken stock or mild
  fish stock, lightly salted*

Salt to taste

Zest of 1 lemon (optional)

*2 pounds mussels, cleaned
  and debearded*

Chopped parsley for garnish

Sauté the garlic, shallots and paprika in oil in a large shallow casserole with a tight-fitting lid; do not brown. Add the rice and sauté until it begins to color. Add the stock, salt and lemon zest; cover, bring to a boil and reduce heat. Cook until the liquid is almost absorbed, about 15 minutes. Add the mussels, replace cover and cook another 5 minutes or so until mussels open. Garnish with chopped parsley.

OCTOPUS

(Octopus spp.)

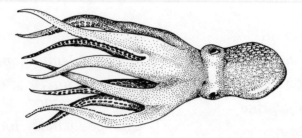

Other Names: *Devilfish, pulpo.*	**Range:** *Temperate and tropical oceans of the world.*
	Season: *All year.*
Description: *Variegated orange to purple skin.*	**Fat Content:** *Low.*
	Yield: *80% meat from smaller species.*
Size: O. punctatus—*15–50 pounds,* O. binoculatus—*to 5 pounds. Smaller sizes more desirable.*	**Available Forms:** *Whole or piece, fresh or cooked.*

Like squid, octopus is a cephalopod. Unlike squid, it requires tenderizing or long, slow cooking.

Octopus is delicious in tomato-based stews, and should be simmered for 20–25 minutes before it is added to the pot. It can be grilled after tenderizing and served with Lemon-Garlic Butter (page 255) or just a squeeze of lemon, or basted with Teriyaki Sauce (page 264) and grilled.

Stewed Octopus with Fennel

Serves 4

1–1½ pounds octopus,
 tentacles and body

1 tablespoon olive oil

1 large yellow onion,
 julienned

2 tablespoons chopped garlic

1 cup fennel bulb, sliced
 ½ inch thick crosswise

½ cup white wine

2 tablespoons chopped
 parsley

2 canned anchovy filets,
 roughly chopped

Cut octopus tentacles and body into ½-inch slices or strips. Blanch in salted water for 5 minutes and allow to cool in liquid, then drain.

Sauté onion, garlic and fennel in oil in a casserole or large saucepan until soft; do not brown. Add octopus, wine, parsley and anchovy; cover and simmer for 30 minutes or longer. Serve in soup bowls with French bread.

OYSTER

Pacific Oyster

(Crassostrea gigas)

Other Names: *Japanese oyster.*

Description: *Bivalve. Elongated, thin shell.*

Size: *2½ inches and up.*

Range: *Pacific coast.*

Season: *All year.*

Fat Content: *Low.*

Available Forms: *Live, shucked, smoked.*

Eastern Oyster

(Crassostrea virginica)

Other Names: *Blue point, Cape Cod, Apalachicola, Chesapeake.*

Description: *Bivalve. Thick and slightly elongated shell with a deep cup.*

Size: *About 3 inches, ideal for the half-shell.*

Range: *Atlantic coast and the Gulf of Mexico.*

Season: *All year.*

Fat Content: *Low.*

Available Forms: *Live, shucked.*

Belon

(Ostrea edulis)

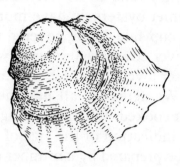

Other Names: *Plate oyster.*

Description: *Bivalve. Flat. Often almost perfectly circular, thin shell.*

Size: *1½–3½ inches.*

Range: *Aquacultured in Moss Landing and Tomales Bay in California, Washington and Maine. Indigenous to France.*

Season: *All year.*

Fat Content: *Low.*

Available Forms: *Live.*

This oyster has a slightly metallic taste. It is delicate and tender, ideal for the half-shell.

Olympia

(Ostrea lurida)

This indigenous western oyster has been over-harvested; whole oysters are available only in Washington state. Shucked Olympia oysters can occasionally be found in West Coast markets.

Oysters vary considerably in taste and appearance according to where they are grown. Blue Point, Cape Cod, Apalachicola and Chesapeake are, in fact, all *Crassostrea virginica;* they vary from bland and tender to salty and firm, according to water temperature, water composition and growing techniques. (For a detailed account of oyster aquaculture in California, see "The California Oyster Story," page 278.)

Oysters spawn in the summer months (the months without an "r") when they tend to be fatty and less desirable for the half-shell. Summer oysters do have more protein, however.

Store oysters cup side down, covered with a damp towel and refrigerated. Never cover oysters with water.

For most oyster lovers, the best way to enjoy them is raw, on the half-shell. We agree for all but the large Pacific oysters, which we prefer cooked. When selecting oysters, the size of the cup is the best indication of the size of the meat.

Oysters can be prepared by a number of methods. Oysters in the shell can be steamed, baked or grilled. Shucked oysters can be stewed, battered and fried, sautéed or skewered and grilled. Several classic preparations such as oysters Rockefeller involve baking them on the half-shell.

The liquid in which oysters have been cooked is called "liquor" and is often used to enrich sauces.

To Shuck an Oyster

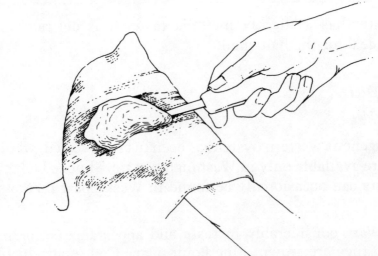

1 Hold the oyster cup side down, using several thicknesses of folded toweling or a potholder to protect your hand. Place the tip of an *oyster knife* (page 18) between the heels of the shells near the hinge, and pry upward. The shell will release with a pop.

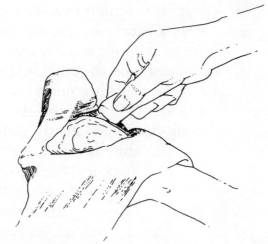

2 Slide the knife in along the top shell, being careful not to
  puncture the oyster. Sever the connector muscle, which is
generally about two-thirds of the way from the hinge to the
end, and remove the top shell.

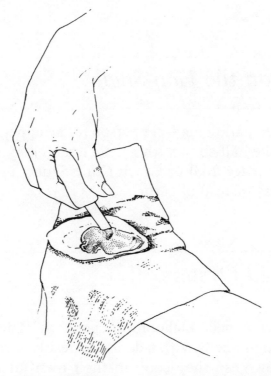

3 Slide the knife under the oyster and sever the bottom muscle. The oyster should now slide around freely in the shell.

4 For certain oysters (especially the Japanese or Pacific variety grown by the cultchless method) that have fragile shells and tend to break at the heel when the above shucking method is used: Find the seam between the shells along the right-hand side; gently slide the tip of the knife between the shells; with a back-and-forth rocking action, work the knife in toward the muscle; proceed as above once the muscle has been reached.

Oysters on the Half-Shell

Shuck oysters, allowing 6 per person for an appetizer. Serve the oysters on the half-shell with a little lemon juice or with Sauce Mignonette (page 263) or Green Chile Sauce (page 264) made with shallots instead of garlic.

Barbecued Oysters

Oysters do not need elaborate preparation. They can be bar-becued in their shells with a delicious result. Grill the oysters, cup side down, so they cook in their own juice. Don't turn them during cooking. They are done when the shells pop open, about 8 minutes. Serve the oysters on the half-shell with any of the following sauces: Beurre Blanc (page 253); Green Chile Sauce (page 264); Fresh Tomato Salsa (page 262); Lemon-Garlic Butter (page 255); Fresh Cilantro Chutney (page 265).

Oysters Bienville
William Marinelli

William Marinelli, a marine biologist and oyster enthusiast, provided the following three recipes as well as most of the information on oyster culture.

Serves 4

24 oysters in the shell	*2 teaspoons curry powder*
1½ cups Fumet (page 252)	*Juice of 1 lemon*
¼ cup olive oil	*Salt to taste*
¼ cup all-purpose flour	*Cayenne to taste*

Preheat the broiler. Scrub the oysters to remove sand and grit.

Steam oysters in a little *fumet* until the shells open. Remove the top shells. Reserve the steaming liquid.

Heat the oil in a heavy saucepan. Add the flour a tablespoon at a time, whisking to combine the oil. When all the flour is added, you should have a thin paste. Add the curry powder and cook over low heat for 3–4 minutes. Do not brown the *roux*. Add the *fumet* and steaming liquid, whisking to form a smooth sauce. Simmer slowly for 5 minutes, add the lemon juice and remove from the heat. Season to taste with salt and cayenne.

Spoon 1 tablespoon of sauce over each oyster. Broil the oysters until heated through, 3–5 minutes. Serve immediately.

Oysters with Pasta

William Marinelli

Serves 4

24 oysters in the shell	1 pound fresh or dry pasta, such as fettucine or linguine
Dry white wine	
1 tablespoon chopped garlic	Chopped parsley
4 tablespoons butter	Grated Parmesan cheese
Juice of 1 lemon	

Scrub oysters to remove sand and grit. Place them in a steamer or heavy pot. Steam the oysters in about ½ inch of white wine until they open, approximately 10 minutes. Set them aside.

Strain the remaining liquid through cheesecloth or a coffee filter. Return the liquid to the pot, add the garlic, butter and lemon juice, and reduce by two thirds.

Cook and drain the pasta. Reheat oysters in the sauce, arrange oysters on the noodles and pour the sauce over the noodles. Sprinkle with parsley and cheese.

Stewed Oysters with Vegetables
William Marinelli

Serves 4

1 pint shucked oysters,
  with liquor

½ cup milk

1 teaspoon lemon juice

¼ teaspoon cayenne

¼ cup olive oil

½ cup onions

1 tablespoon chopped garlic

¼ cup finely diced carrots

½ cup finely diced celery

½ cup finely diced
  mushrooms

¼ cup grated Parmesan
  cheese

2 tablespoons chopped parsley

Marinate the oysters in the milk, lemon juice and cayenne for 30 minutes.

In a skillet large enough to hold all the ingredients, sauté the onions and garlic in the olive oil until the onions are soft. Add the carrots and celery. When the carrots are nearly cooked, add the mushrooms. Cook briefly, then add the oysters and their marinade. Cook over medium heat for 3–5 minutes, depending on the size of the oysters.

Serve over pasta or rice, garnished with Parmesan cheese and parsley.

Oyster Loaf

This recipe is a popular entrée at the Gulf coast Oyster Bar in Oakland, which features seafood flown in from the Gulf and prepared in the cooking styles of New Orleans. In Louisiana this sandwich is also called an Oyster Po' Boy.

Serves 4

24 small oysters, shucked

Milk to cover (about 1 cup)

2 teaspoons Pernod or other anise liquor

Oil for frying

Zatarain's Fish Fry (available in many gourmet shops) or fine cornmeal

1 loaf French bread, cut in half lengthwise and hollowed out so that little more than crust remains

2 cups shredded romaine

½ cup Creole Mayonnaise (page 258)

Marinate the oysters in milk and Pernod for at least 30 minutes. Drain the oysters and pat dry.

Heat the oil to 375° in a wok or large pot. Coat the oysters with Fish Fry or cornmeal. Fry them in oil until they are golden brown. Drain on paper towels. While the oysters are cooking, toast the French bread. To make a sandwich, moisten both halves of the bread with mayonnaise. Cover one half with shredded romaine and the other half with the oysters. Cut the sandwich into quarters and serve while the oysters are still hot.

Broiled Eggplant Stuffed with Oysters

This dish is rich and satisfying, though not as caloric as it tastes. It can be served hot or warm.

Serves 8 as an appetizer   Serves 4 as a main course

2 large eggplants

4 tablespoons oil

2 medium yellow onions, chopped

2-3 tablespoons chopped garlic

1 cup bread crumbs

¼ cup chopped parsley

1 teaspoon fresh thyme or other herbs

1 pound shucked oysters

½ cup grated Parmesan cheese

Cayenne to taste

Juice of 1 lemon

Slice the eggplants in half lengthwise. Broil them until soft, 8–10 minutes. Remove the pulp with a spoon without cutting through the skin. Cut the pulp into 1-inch dice.

In a large skillet, sauté the onions and garlic in oil until soft. Add the eggplant pulp, bread crumbs, parsley, thyme and oysters. Stir and cook for 1 minute. Remove from heat and add cheese, cayenne and lemon juice.

Preheat the broiler. Fill each eggplant half with a generous amount of the stuffing. Broil until the bread crumbs brown, about 5 minutes.

Oyster Stuffing for Fish

Usc this stuffing for large, boneless pieces of firm fish, such as grouper, boned sections of large fish, or small whole fish such as pan-sized salmon.

Yield: About 1½ cups

1 tablespoon butter or oil

1 teaspoon chopped garlic

1 scallion, finely chopped

½ pint shucked oysters,
  with liquor

¼ cup bread crumbs

2 teaspoons chopped parsley

Sauté garlic and scallion in butter until cooked. If using small oysters such as Olympias, add them whole; otherwise, chop the oysters into ½-inch or smaller pieces and add them with their liquor. Add the bread crumbs and parsley and cook gently until the liquid is absorbed. Season to taste. Allow to cool before stuffing fish.

PERIWINKLE

(Family Littorinidae)

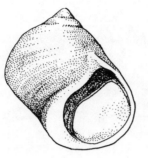

Description: *Univalve. Small, grey. Usually found in large colonies.*	**Season:** *All year. Abundant in summer months.*
Size: *½ inch and up.*	**Fat Content:** *Low.*
Range: *Some species exist along all the coast of the United States.*	**Available Forms:** *Live.*

Periwinkles are popular here primarily among Italian and Asian communities. They will probably become better known as beachcombers seeking mussels and clams discover the culinary possibilities of these abundant shellfish.

Scrub the shells to remove sand and grit. Boil in salted water for 10 minutes or until the operculum (plastic-like shield covering the open end) opens. The meat can be removed with a toothpick or, better still, an unfolded paper clip. Dip periwinkles in Lemon-Garlic Butter (page 255) or Aioli (page 260). Or, substitute boiled periwinkles for steamed clams in Clams in Black Bean Sauce (page 92).

REDFISH

(Sciaenops ocellata)

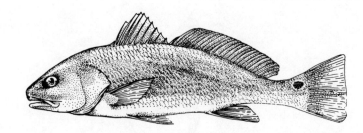

Other Names: *Red drum, channel bass, red bass.*	**Range:** *Southern Atlantic and Gulf coasts.*
Description: *Metallic rosy gold fading to silver. Large scales. Red pectoral fins. One or more black spots on tail.*	**Season:** *All year. Most common warmer months.*
	Fat Content: *Low.*
Size: *3–10 pounds. Smaller fish more desirable.*	**Yield:** *33% filet.*
	Available Forms: *Round, filet.*

This mainstay of New Orleans fish cookery is a member of the croaker family which also includes the white seabass and corbina. As Louisiana-style restaurants become more popular in other parts of the country, including California, redfish and other Gulf specialties are being more widely distributed.

Use redfish interchangeably with striped bass, white seabass, corbina and sea trout. Broiled or grilled redfish filets are delicious with Red Hollandaise Sauce (page 256) or oyster sauce (see Seabass with Oyster Sauce, page 198).

RED SNAPPER

(Lutjanus campechanus)

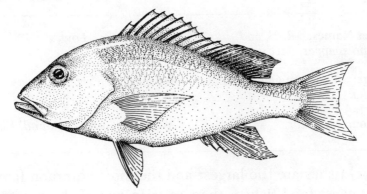

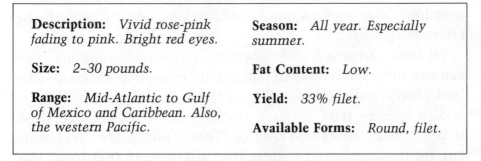

Description: *Vivid rose-pink fading to pink. Bright red eyes.*	**Season:** *All year. Especially summer.*
Size: *2–30 pounds.*	**Fat Content:** *Low.*
Range: *Mid-Atlantic to Gulf of Mexico and Caribbean. Also, the western Pacific.*	**Yield:** *33% filet.* **Available Forms:** *Round, filet.*

The fact that a wide range of Pacific rockfishes have been marketed as "red snapper" is a testament to the quality of this fish. Several other species of *Lutjanus,* including the grey and blackfin snappers, are caught commercially, but red snapper is the most valuable and desirable. Eastern snapper is occasionally available on the West Coast at a premium price; to distinguish it from the local pretenders, it is likely to be labeled "true red snapper." California regulations will probably continue to allow certain rockfish species to be sold as "Pacific snapper," but "red snapper" should refer only to the real thing.

This versatile and delicious fish is suitable to any cooking method. Most classic recipes from the Gulf and Caribbean regions calling for a firm white fish were originally developed for this species.

Alternatives: *Grouper (A,G,P), black sea bass (A), striped bass (A,P), fancy rockfish.*

ROCKFISH

(Sebastes spp.)

Other Names: *Rock cod, Pacific snapper, "red snapper."*	**Fat Content:** *Low.*
Range: *Southern California to Alaska.*	**Yield:** *30–40% filet, depending on size and body shape.*
Season: *All year.*	**Available Forms:** *Round, filet.*

The rockfishes are the largest and the most common family of Pacific coast food fishes; they are also one of the most varied and confusing. In terms of cooking quality, they may be grouped into four categories as represented below, beginning with the choicest species.

Without carrying a technical field guide in the market, you can use a few guidelines in judging an unfamiliar rockfish. The best general indicator of quality is the overall shape: the deeper-bodied species tend to have firmer and better-flavored flesh than the more elongated species. This is not to say that bocaccio, for instance, is an undesirable fish, simply that its milder flavor and softer flesh is not appropriate to certain cooking methods.

There is also a strong correlation between quality and price. Chinese fish markets often display half a dozen species, the most expensive being three times the price of the cheapest. (Incidentally, the more choice species tend to be "loners" rather than school fish, which adds to their market price.)

Rockfish in the first two categories are excellent and suitable for virtually any cooking method. Their flesh is firm enough to approach real snapper in both flavor and texture. These varieties are definitely superior for Chinese recipes for steamed or fried whole fish. Where a recipe or alternative calls for "fancy rockfish," choose one from these two categories.

Yellowtails, blues and blacks are fairly common in the market. Their flesh is firm enough for fileting and grilling, but slightly less flavorful than the fancy varieties. Filets of bocaccio and its equivalents, however, are difficult to handle as they tend to fall apart easily. For these varieties, baking whole fish in a sauce and other moist-heat methods are preferable to grilling or sautéing; filets may also be broiled with a compound butter, as in Broiled Sablefish with Anchovy Butter (page 183).

Bolina
(S. auriculatus)

Other Names: *Brown rockfish, sand bass.*	**Size:** *To 5 pounds.*
Description: *Brown, mottled with orange-brown.*	**Similar Species:** *Gopher rockfish* (S. carnatus), *copper or barriga* (S. caurinus), *China* (S. nebulosus).

Goldeneye Rockfish
(S. ruberrimus)

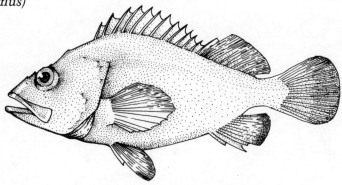

Other Names: *Yelloweye, turkey red rockfish.*	**Size:** *To 10 pounds.*
Description: *Bright pink, black tips on fins. Yellow eye.*	**Similar Species:** *Flag or tree* (S. rubrivinctus), *canary or fantail rockfish* (S. pinniger).

Yellowtail Rockfish
(S. flavidus)

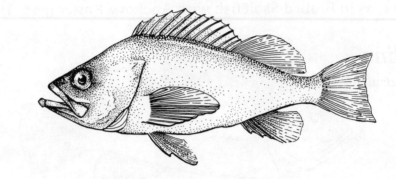

Description: *Olivaceous to brown. Bright yellow fins and tail.* **Size:** *1–4 pounds.*	**Similar Species:** *Black* (S. melanops), *blue* (S. mystinus), *vermillion* (S miniatus).

Bocaccio
(S. paucispinis)

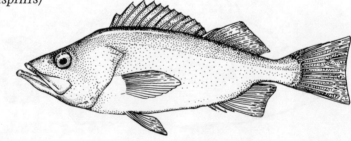

Description: *Dusky red fading to pinkish. Mouth opens above eye.* **Size:** *1–20 pounds (mostly under 5 pounds).*	**Similar Species:** *Chilipepper* (S. goodei), *widow* (S. entomelas), *shortbelly* (S. jordani), *strawberry* (S. elongatus).

Baked Rockfish Veracruz Style

Huachinango á la Veracruzana is perhaps Mexico's most famous seafood dish. Around the Gulf of Mexico it is made with red snapper. On the West Coast, snapper is an expensive luxury, but the local rockfish makes a more than adequate substitute. In fact, any firm-fleshed white fish will do. Instructions are given below both for dressed fish and filets.

Serves 4

1 4–5-pound rockfish (yellowtail or better), dressed, or 2 smaller fish or 1½-2 pounds filets

Juice of 1 lemon or lime

Salt

2 tablespoons olive oil

1 medium onion, julienned

1 bell pepper, julienned

1 tablespoon chopped garlic

2 medium tomatoes, peeled, seeded and roughly chopped or 1 small can peeled tomatoes

¼ cup sliced green olives

1 tablespoon capers

1 or 2 pickled chile peppers (jalapeños or serranos en escabeche, *available canned at Latin American groceries*)

Preheat oven to 450°.

Sprinkle fish with lemon or lime juice and salt, and set aside. Sauté onion, pepper, garlic and tomatoes in olive oil until just softened; do not brown. (If using canned tomatoes, add them after the onion and pepper are soft.) Simmer sauce until most of the liquid is evaporated.

For whole fish: place fish in an oiled deep baking pan. Pour the sauce over the fish and scatter the olives, capers and chiles on top. Cover the pan with a tight-fitting lid or foil and bake 10 minutes to the inch, or until flesh flakes easily from the tail. Serve with the accumulated sauce from the pan.

For filets: cut into individual portions, place on squares of foil or baking paper as for Baked Lingcod with Tapenade (page 140), top with sauce, olives, capers and chiles, seal edges and bake 8–10 minutes.

Grilled Rockfish Yúcatan Style

This is the traditional treatment for grilled fish in the Yúcatan. There, it is typically used for *cazón* (a small dogfish), but it is well suited to any type of shark as well as rockfish.

Alternatives: *Shark*   *Serves 4*

1 tablespoon achiote *(page 36)*

¼ teaspoon black peppercorns

¼ teaspoon oregano

¼ teaspoon cumin, whole

2-3 cloves garlic, peeled

½ teaspoon paprika

Pinch cayenne

Juice of: 1 lemon, 1 lime, 1 orange and 1 small grapefruit

1½ pounds rockfish filet (yellowtail or better)

Grind the whole spices in a spice grinder. Transfer them to a blender jar, add the remaining ingredients and blend to a smooth paste. Spread the paste on the filets and set aside for several hours to season.

Grill the fish until just done. Serve with lemon or lime wedges and rice. Or, serve with warm tortillas, Black Bean Paste (next page) and Fresh Tomato Salsa (page 262), letting each person make tacos.

Black Bean Paste

This bean paste is appropriate for any seafood or other burrito.

½ pound black (turtle) beans

5 cups water

½ onion, peeled and stuck with a few cloves

A few ounces bacon or ham trimmings, pork rind or a pork bone

½ teaspoon dried summer savory, or a large sprig of fresh

2–3 small dried chiles or 1 large dried chile such as ancho

Salt to taste

2–3 tablespoons chicken or duck fat or lard

Check the beans for pebbles or other foreign objects. In a large heavy saucepan or casserole, cover the beans by at least an inch with water. Add the remaining ingredients except the salt and fat. Bring to a boil, cover and reduce heat. Simmer until the beans are fully cooked, adding more water if necessary to prevent them from drying out. Season to taste. (Beans may be prepared to this point a day or two ahead and refrigerated.)

Purée the beans, together with their broth, through a food mill or in a blender or food processor. (Use care if blending hot beans.) Heat the fat in a large skillet and fry the bean mixture, stirring to prevent sticking, until a thick paste is formed.

Hot Pickled Rockfish

Pescado en Escabeche

Alternatives: *Any firm white-fleshed fish*   *Serves 6–8 as an appetizer*

1 pound rockfish filet
  (yellowtail or better) at
  room temperature

Salt

Juice of 1 lemon or lime

1 teaspoon black peppercorns

½ teaspoon coriander seed

½ teaspoon cumin seed

2 cloves or ¼ teaspoon
  ground cloves

2 allspice or ¼ teaspoon
  allspice powder

12 cloves garlic, peeled

½ cup wine vinegar

½ cup water

¼ teaspoon cinnamon

½ teaspoon oregano

1 or 2 bay leaves

1-2 teaspoons salt

½ teaspoon sugar

1 red onion, sliced thin for
  garnish

Season the filets with salt and lemon or lime juice and set aside. Grind the whole spices in a blender or spice grinder. Press two of the cloves of garlic into a skillet; add the ground spices, water and vinegar and bring to a boil. Add the remaining ingredients and simmer for a few minutes.

Slice the fish into bite-size pieces. Arrange them in a serving dish, and pour over the vinegar mixture. The heat of the liquid should be enough to cook the fish.

Serve warm or cold, garnished with red onion slices.

Steamed Rockfish with Fresh Herbs

Bruce Cost

This is a variation on the classic Cantonese approach to whole fish. Use the best rockfish available.

Alternatives: *Small striped bass (A,P), snapper (A,G), black sea bass (A)*
Serves 3–4 as a main course

2½–3-pound fancy rockfish, cleaned, with head on

⅓ cup oil

⅓ cup finely shredded ginger

1 cup finely shredded scallions

⅓ cup finely shredded red or green peppers or mild chile peppers such as Anaheim

1 cup chicken stock

Salt to taste

½ teaspoon white pepper

1 tablespoon cornstarch dissolved in ¼ cup water

Cilantro for garnish

Rinse and dry the fish.

Steam it on a plate for 15–20 minutes (page 64) or until the thickest part is easily pierced with a skewer. Transfer the fish to a warm serving platter. Meanwhile, heat the oil in a saucepan to near smoking. Scatter the ginger, half the scallions and half the peppers over the fish. Start the stock boiling. When the oil is hot, pour it over the fish. Add salt and pepper to the stock and thicken it with the cornstarch mixture. Pour the sauce over the fish. Scatter the rest of the vegetables on top. Garnish with cilantro and serve.

Seafood Hot Pot with Fish Balls

This dish takes its name from its method of presentation. A large pot of seafood, noodles and vegetables is kept warm at the table as each diner helps himself to several servings in small rice bowls. In Chinese restaurants it is served in a vessel known as a fire pot or hot pot, but a large chafing dish or fondue pot will do.

Serves 10 or more as a side dish

3 quarts rich chicken stock (reduce regular chicken stock by half)

18 or so Fish Balls (below)

½ pound Chinese cabbage, chopped

¼ pound transparent Chinese vermicelli (available in Asian groceries)

Serves 6 as a main course

½ pound medium or large shrimp, peeled

½ pound sea scallops

½ pound shucked oysters, with their liquor

¼ cup cilantro

Bring the chicken stock to a boil in a pot large enough to hold all the ingredients. Add the fish balls and cabbage and cook for about 5 minutes. Add the rest of the ingredients and cook until the shellfish are done, about 3 minutes longer.

Transfer the seafood and liquid to a preheated hot pot or fondue dish. Garnish with cilantro. Serve in bowls and pass soy sauce, white vinegar and a hot sauce such as Chinese hot chili oil or Tabasco sauce.

Fish Balls

Inexpensive varieties of rockfish are often used to make Chinese-style fish balls.

1 pound rockfish filet   *1 teaspoon grated ginger*
4–6 tablespoons ice water

Grind the fish filets with a meat grinder or chop them by hand until you have a smooth, thick paste. Add the ice water a tablespoon at a time and then mix in the ginger.

Fill a small bowl with ice water. Form the paste into balls about 1½ inches in diameter, dipping your fingers into the water frequently. (The moisture keeps the fish from sticking to your fingers and the cool temperature helps the balls stick together.)

Refrigerate the fish balls for at least 1 hour so they will hold together during cooking.

California "Bouillabaisse"

Since rockfish is so plentiful, cheap and easy to filet (the bones and head are good for stock, too), it is the logical base for a California fisherman's stew. However, many other varieties of fish can be used (page 180).

Of all seafood dishes, none has as many "authentic" versions, each with its own loyal followers, as that Mediterranean standby, bouillabaisse. Rather than enter the debate, we have qualified our version both with quotation marks and the California appellation, so no enraged Marseillais can accuse us of putting forth a bastard version of his favorite dish. Besides, we think it's pretty good.

A variety of saltwater fish is one key to a good bouillabaisse. Bear in mind that this dish, like all fisherman's stews, began as a way of cooking the day's catch. Don't be afraid to improvise, or to throw in some of the stranger varieties in the fish market. A few guidelines, however, are in order:

A variety of textures is desirable. For example, combine a firm, coarse-fleshed fish such as rockfish with a finer-textured flounder or sole and a dense, meaty-textured angler or shark.

Strongly flavored fish such as mackerel will easily dominate the dish. Use them sparingly if at all. On the other hand, the robust tomato and garlic flavors of the broth will do nothing for more fine-flavored fish such as salmon or snapper.

Shellfish add flavor and texture variety as well as color. Mussels, clams and even shrimp and crab would be welcome additions.

Serves 6

2 tablespoons olive oil

½ cup diced leek tops or scallion tops or yellow onion

4–6 cloves garlic, chopped

¼ cup chopped fennel leaves or ¼ teaspoon fennel seeds

2 pounds ripe tomatoes, chopped, or 1 large can tomatoes, drained

2 quarts water

2–3 pounds fish heads and bones, well rinsed

2-inch strip of orange peel

Pinch of saffron

Bouquet garni of celery, thyme, bay, parsley and marjoram or oregano

1–1½ pounds boneless fish and shellfish (see above suggestions)

½ cup Rouille (page 261)

In a large kettle or stockpot, heat the oil and gently sauté the leek tops, garlic and fennel without browning. Add the tomatoes (juice, seeds and all), stir and cook a few minutes to evaporate some of the liquid. Add the fish heads and bones and water, bring to a boil, reduce heat and skim any scum from the surface. Add the orange peel, saffron and *bouquet garni* and simmer 45 minutes. Strain the liquid, discard the bones and vegetables and return the stock to the pot.

Add the fish and shellfish to the simmering stock in the order of their required cooking times: 8–10 minutes for clams in the shell or uncooked crab; 6 minutes or so for dense fish such as angler; 4–5 minutes for mussels, most other fish and cooked crab; and about 3 minutes for thin filets of flatfish.

Serve in shallow bowls with French bread, stirring in *rouille* to taste.

Baked Stuffed Rockfish

Alternatives: *Speckled trout, small snapper (A,G) or grouper (A,G,P)*

Serves 3–4 as a main course

4 tablespoons olive oil

1 green bell pepper, chopped

1 medium yellow onion, chopped

2 serrano or other fresh hot chiles, chopped

2 tablespoons chopped garlic

3 tomatoes, peeled, seeded and chopped or 1 cup canned tomatoes

¼ cup cilantro

1–1½ cups cooked white or brown rice

Salt and pepper to taste

1 2½–3-pound rockfish (yellowtail or comparable species), dressed or boned

Lemon wedges for garnish

Preheat oven to 400°.

Sauté the bell pepper, onion, chiles and garlic in olive oil. When the onion is translucent, add the tomatoes and cilantro. Cook another minute, combine with rice and season to taste with salt and pepper. Transfer the stuffing to a bowl to cool.

Stuff the body and head of the fish. Wrap it in foil and seal carefully. Bake for 25–30 minutes, or until done by the skewer test. Remove the stuffing from the fish. Arrange on a tray with the fish in the center, surrounded by the stuffing and the lemon wedges.

SABLEFISH

(Anoplopoma fimbria)

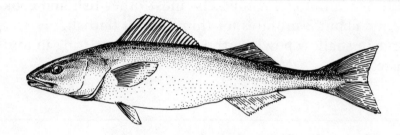

Other Names: *Black cod, butterfish (filets only).*	**Season:** *All year.*
	Yield: *40% filet.*
Description: *Black fading to grey.*	
	Fat Content: *High.*
Size: *1–15 pounds.*	**Available Forms:** *Filet, round, smoked, chunk.*
Range: *Northern Pacific (well offshore).*	

"Butterfish" filets are widely available in supermarkets as well as fish markets. While not suited to every method, it can be delicious if properly cooked. Broiling with a well-flavored compound butter is the best dry-heat method. With its mild flavor, sablefish is ideal for curries and other highly seasoned stews and braised dishes.

Broiled Sablefish with Anchovy Butter

Alternatives: *Lingcod   Serves 4*

*4 filets of sablefish, about
  6 ounces each*

*2 ounces Anchovy Butter
(page 254)*

Arrange the filets, skin side down, on a lightly buttered roasting pan. Spread the tops with anchovy butter. Broil for 3–5 minutes, depending on thickness. When done, the thick end of the filet should be just about to flake. Transfer the filets to plates with a long spatula and drizzle with any butter remaining in the pan.

Curried Sablefish with Spinach

The mild flavor of sablefish is a nice foil for aromatic curry spices and garlic. This dish is easy to prepare, although the finished product looks elaborate.

Alternatives: *Sculpin,
  tilefish (A)*

*Serves 2 as a main course
Serves 4 or more as a side dish*

2 tablespoons oil

*1 medium yellow onion,
  chopped*

1 tablespoon chopped garlic

¼ teaspoon ground turmeric

¼ teaspoon ground coriander

Pinch of cloves

Pinch of cinnamon

Cayenne to taste

½ pound sablefish filet

*½ pound spinach, washed,
  drained and chopped*

*2 tomatoes, peeled, seeded
  and diced, or 2 canned
  tomatoes, chopped*

Sauté the onion and garlic in the oil until onion is translucent. Add the spices. Cook over low heat for 2 minutes. Add the fish, spinach, tomatoes and a little water to make a thick sauce. Cook over medium heat until the fish is done.

Fresh Cilantro Chutney (page 265) is a wonderful accompaniment to this and other fish curries.

SALMON

King Salmon

(Oncorhynchus tshawytscha)

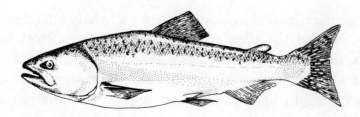

Other Names: *Chinook.*	**Season:** *Spring–fall.*
Description: *Dark blue fading to silver. Black spots dorsally and on tail. Black gums.*	**Fat Content:** *High.*
	Yield: *Up to 67% filet.*
Size: *6–25 pounds and up.*	**Available Forms:** *Dressed, chunk, steak, filet, dry smoked, cured.*
Range: *Pacific coast and rivers from central California north.*	

Silver Salmon

(Onchorhynchus kisutch)

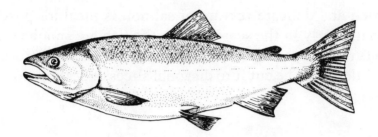

Other Names: *Coho.*	**Season:** *Spring–fall.*
Description: *Similar to the king but with fewer spots. White gums.*	**Fat Content:** *High.*
	Yield: *Up to 67% filet.*
Size: *4–10 pounds. Aquacultured to 1 pound.*	**Available Forms:** *Dressed, chunk, steak, filet, dry smoked, cured.*
Range: *Pacific coast and rivers from central California north.*	

King is the most desirable salmon species. However, despite strict management of sport and commercial fisheries, the population has been steadily declining.

Silver is second only to the king in quality. It commands a slightly lower wholesale price, which may or may not be reflected in the retail price. (Know what you are buying—check the gums.)

These two species and the red or sockeye, pink and chum salmons make up the most valuable fish resource on the Pacific coast. They also provide some of the best eating. The rich, flavorful and distinctively colored flesh of salmon is suitable for almost any cooking method. It is particularly delicious grilled or broiled, baked with or without stuffing or poached and served hot or cold.

Alternatives: *Atlantic salmon, steelhead.*

Poached Salmon

The rich and delicate texture of salmon is ideal for poaching, especially early in the season when the fish are smaller. Steaks or filets may be poached according to the same basic procedure. Thick filets may be cut into diagonal slices or scallops for easier poaching.

Serves 4

1–1½ pounds filet of salmon   *½ cup sauce (see below)*
  or 4 6–8-ounce steaks

1–2 quarts Court-Bouillon
  (page 251) or Fumet
  (page 252)

Arrange the salmon pieces in a single layer in an oiled flame-proof casserole, baking dish or a skillet. In a saucepan, heat the liquid until just simmering. Carefully pour the liquid over the fish. Simmer over low to medium heat, but do not allow the liquid to boil. Thin scallops will be done in 2–3 minutes, while thick steaks may take up to 8–10 minutes. When done, remove the fish with a slotted spatula, drain well and transfer to a warm platter or individual plates. Before adding sauce, blot away any remaining liquid from the plates with a towel.

Serve poached salmon with Beurre Blanc (page 253), Béarnaise Sauce (page 257) or another hollandaise-type sauce. Cold poached salmon is generally served with a flavored mayonnaise (pages 257–59).

Grilled Salmon with Fennel

By midsummer, ocean salmon become firmer and fuller-flavored, and are more suitable for grilling than poaching.

Serves 4

1 large or *2 small fennel bulbs (about ½ pound)*	*Coarse ground black pepper to taste*
4 *6–8-ounce salmon steaks*	*Beurre Blanc (page 253)*
3 tablespoons olive oil	

Trim the fennel bulbs, reserving the leaves and tender stems. Slice the bulbs lengthwise in half or into ½-inch slices. Blanch them in salted water for 30 seconds or until they soften slightly. Rinse them with cold water to stop the cooking. Marinate the fennel slices and salmon in olive oil and pepper for at least 1 hour.

Grill the fennel slices on one side. When they are lightly browned, turn them and add the salmon to the grill. A ¾-inch steak will be cooked rare in about 6 minutes over a hot charcoal fire and well done in 8 minutes. Baste the steaks with the marinade while grilling. When the fennel is tender, remove it to a warm platter or serving plates. Serve the fish and fennel with a Beurre Blanc to which have been added finely chopped fennel leaves and stems.

Grilled Salmon with Cilantro Cream Sauce

Carol Brendlinger

Serves 4

4 6–8-ounce salmon steaks	1 quart cream
2 tablespoons olive oil	2 tablespoons Crème Fraiche
½ cup cilantro	(page 39)
2 quarts Fumet (page 252)	Salt and pepper to taste
¼ cup chopped shallots	Cilantro for garnish
2 cups dry white wine	

Marinate the salmon in olive oil and half the cilantro for 1–4 hours.

Add the shallots to the *fumet* and reduce to 2 cups. Add the white wine and reduce slowly to ½ cup. In a separate saucepan reduce the cream by half. Strain the *fumet* into the cream. Add the *crème fraiche*. Simmer and whisk until the sauce thickens, about 2 minutes. Chop the remaining cilantro, add to the sauce and season to taste. Simmer for 1 minute. Keep the sauce warm over a double boiler or on the edge of the grill.

Grill the salmon. Serve it on a heated platter covered with the sauce. Garnish with cilantro.

Grilled Salmon and Scallop Brochettes

Salmon and scallops are nearly identical in density, and cook at the same rate. Grilling them together on skewers makes for a delightful combination of color and flavor. Use either bay or sea scallops, and cut salmon filet into pieces of similar size. Serve with Beurre Blanc (page 253) or a simple herb butter (page 255).

Gravlax

This is a classic Scandinavian recipe for curing salmon. It requires no special equipment or ingredient, only what you would usually have on hand in the kitchen. You can make it from two filets of a small salmon and use the quantities given here or cut the recipe in half and use two smaller filets.

Serves 40–50 as an appetizer

A 6–8-pound salmon or steelhead (or chunk from a larger fish)

½ cup coarse (kosher) salt

5 tablespoons sugar

1 teaspoon white pepper

2 tablespoons fresh chopped dill

Parsley, cucumber slices, red bell pepper slices for garnish

Filet the salmon, leaving the skin on. Combine salt, sugar and pepper and rub the filets with this mixture.

Lay one filet on top of the other, thick width to thin width. Wrap wax paper and then foil around the filets. Place the wrapped fish on a plate and place another plate on top. Rest a weight of about 2 pounds on the top plate to maintain firm contact between the filets. Refrigerate for 4–5 days.

To serve, cut the *gravlax* into thin strips and arrange in a circular pattern on a small serving tray. Decorate the center with parsley, cucumber slices and/or red bell pepper slices.

Smoked Salmon "Mousse"
Victoria Fahey

Victoria Fahey of Curds and Whey in Oakland provided this delicious creamy salmon recipe. It should be made with salmon that has been dry-smoked rather than a wet-cured lox. Serve chilled or at room temperature with crackers or rye bread.

Alternatives: *Smoked trout*   *Serves 18 as an appetizer*

1 pound smoked salmon,
    skinned and well trimmed

1 pound sweet butter

2 tablespoons tomato paste

¼ cup lemon juice

¼ teaspoon ground mace

½ teaspoon fresh ground
    black pepper

¼ cup capers

½–1 cup sour cream or
    Crème Fraîche (page 39)

Additional capers or thinly
    sliced lemon for garnish

Cut the salmon into 1-inch cubes. Whip the butter until soft in an electric mixer. Slowly add the salmon, tomato paste, mace and black pepper. Mix on medium speed until the ingredients are fairly smooth but not completely homogenized. Spoon the mousse into a medium-sized serving bowl. Add the capers and toss the mixture gently with a spoon. Serve immediately or refrigerate.

Just before you serve, cover the mousse with a thin layer of sour cream. Garnish with capers or thin slices of lemon.

SAND DAB

(Citarichthys sordidus)

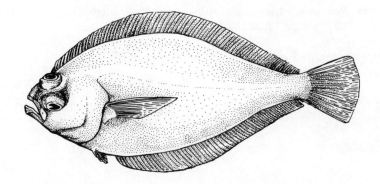

Description: *Brown with orange-black mottling.*	**Season:** *All year.*
	Fat Content: *Low.*
Size: *To 1 pound. 4–8 ounces typical.*	**Yield:** *50% pan-dressed.*
Range: *Southern California to Alaska.*	**Available Forms:** *Round, pan-dressed.*

This small flatfish is one of the most popular selections at San Francisco's old (and new) fish grills. The intense heat of the charcoal crisps the skin while the sweet flesh stays moist due to contact with the bones. Marinades are not really needed or desirable—just a little Beurre Blanc (page 253), a simple herb butter (page 255) or a squeeze of lemon juice.

Sand dabs are also frequently prepared *meuniere* (page 218) or in a bread crumb batter.

Sautéed Sand Dabs with Bread Crumb Batter

Alternatives: *Rex sole, other small soles, surfperch, butterfish,*   *Serves 2*
freshwater "pan fish"

*1½–2 pounds sand dabs,
  round*

Salt and pepper to taste

Flour

1 egg, beaten

¼ cup milk

½ cup or more bread crumbs

*1–2 tablespoons clarified
  butter (see below)*

Juice of ½ lemon

Pan-dress the fish, season them lightly and set them aside. Combine the egg and milk in a shallow bowl. Dredge each fish in flour, then dip in the egg mixture and roll in the bread crumbs until thoroughly coated. (Try to work with just one hand in the egg mixture, keeping the other free to handle the finished product.)

Heat the butter in a large skillet. Sauté the fish, regulating the heat so that the batter does not get too brown. To test for doneness, try to slip a skewer between the filets and the bones from the head end. If it penetrates easily, the fish is done. Transfer the fish to a heated serving platter or plates, add the lemon juice to the remaining butter in the pan and pour over the fish.

To Clarify Butter:

In a small saucepan melt ¼ pound or more of butter over very low heat. Do not allow the butter to boil. The butter fat will separate from the whey and milk solids. Skim any floating solids from the surface and discard. Ladle the butter fat out of the pan, leaving the whey behind. Clarified butter may be stored in a tightly closed jar, refrigerated.

SCALLOP

Sea Scallop
(P. magellicanus)

Description: *Similar to bay scallop. Larger in size and slightly less symmetrical and flatter.*	**Season:** *All year. More abundant in the summer.*
	Fat Content: *Low.*
Size: *5 inches across.*	**Yield:** *15–40 per pound, shucked.*
Range: *Mid-Atlantic to New England.*	**Available Forms:** *Shucked, occasionally live.*

Bay Scallop
(Pecten irradians)

Description: *Symmetrical bivalve. Cream with light brown, pink or light yellow mottling.*	**Season:** *Locally regulated. Generally available fall and winter.*
	Fat Content: *Low.*
Size: *2 inches across.*	**Yield:** *Approximately 90–100 per pound, shucked.*
Range: *Shallow bay waters and salt ponds of the Atlantic and Gulf coasts.*	**Available Forms:** *Shucked, live (infrequently).*

The scallop is the only free-swimming mollusc. It cannot hold its shell together tightly and dies quickly out of water. It is shucked as a matter of course.

In America we eat only the abductor muscle, the large muscle which connects the shells; in Europe the muscle and roe or the entire scallop is eaten.

The bay scallop is a delight and rare on the Pacific coast. Most of what are sold here as bay scallops are small deep-sea scallops from Florida known as calico scallops *(Argopecten gibbus)*.

The larger sea scallop is the most widely available scallop and the basis of the commercial fishery. When fresh, sea scallops are excellent in flavor and texture and are suitable to a wider variety of cooking methods and ingredients than the more delicate bay scallop. Sea scallops make delicious Ceviche (page 70). They are frequently used in fish stuffings and mousse mixtures. Bay scallops are best simply sautéed or poached with a cream-based sauce.

Grilled Scallops with Bacon

Alternatives: *Large oysters*   *Serves 4*

4 slices of bacon
1 pound sea scallops (if larger
   than 1 ounce each, cut in
   half across the grain)

Juice of 1 lemon

Blanch the bacon in boiling water for 3 minutes to remove some of the fat and to partially cook it.

Using small wooden or metal skewers, pierce one end of the bacon then skewer a scallop. Weave in the bacon and add another scallop. Fill the skewers, alternating bacon and scallops.

Grill 3–4 minutes over hot charcoal, or a little longer under a broiler, turning the scallops once. Serve on the skewers with a squeeze of lemon juice.

Sichuan Scallops

The spicy hot flavor of this sauce enhances rather than over-whelms the sweet taste of the scallops.

Alternatives: *Shrimp or prawns*

Serves 4 or more as a side dish
Serves 2 as a main course

1 egg white

½ pound sea scallops cut in half across the grain

2 tablespoons chicken stock

1 tablespoon Sichuan bean paste (page 43)

1 tablespoon dry sherry or rice wine

1 teaspoon soy sauce

2 tablespoons oil

1–2 tablespoons chopped garlic

2 teaspoons chopped ginger

1 stalk celery cut into ¼-inch slices

Beat the egg white until frothy. Toss the scallops in the egg white and refrigerate them.

In a small bowl, combine the stock, bean paste, sherry and soy sauce.

Drain the excess egg white from the scallops with paper towels. Heat the oil in a large skillet or wok. Sauté the garlic and ginger for 10 seconds over high heat. Add the celery and scallops and stir-fry for 30 seconds. Add the sauce mixture and continue cooking until the scallops are heated through, about 1 minute. Serve with rice.

Fried Sea Scallops

Alternatives: *Oysters, mussels*   *Serves 2*

1 egg
1 tablespoon milk
Pinch of salt and pepper
¼ cup all-purpose flour
½ cup fine bread crumbs

½ pound sea scallops (if larger than 1 ounce, slice in half across the grain)
2 cups or more oil for frying

Beat the egg, milk, salt and pepper together. Dip each scallop into flour, shaking off the excess. Dip in egg mixture and coat thoroughly with bread crumbs.

In a heavy pot or wok, heat the oil to 350°. Add the scallops and cook until nicely browned, 3–4 minutes. Drain on paper towels.

Fried scallops are delicious served simply with lemon wedges. If a sauce is desired, try Fines Herbes Mayonnaise (page 258), Tartar Sauce (page 259) or Skordalia (page 260).

WHITE SEABASS

(Cynoscion nobilis)

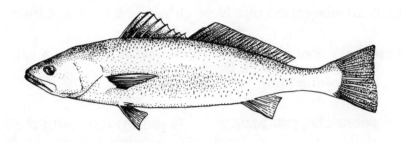

Description: *Blue-grey fading to silver. Large, heavy scales.*

Size: *To 80 pounds. 10–15 pounds more typical.*

Range: *Baja to central California.*

Season: *Spring–summer.*

Fat Content: *Moderate.*

Yield: *40% filet, 65% steak.*

Available Forms: *Pan-dressed, steak, filet, block.*

White seabass is the species traditionally sold as "sea bass" in California. It is now relatively scarce and expensive, but worth seeking out for its fine flavor and texture. Like the other croakers and striped bass, which it resembles in flavor, white seabass is ideal for grilling and broiling, but tends to dry out if overcooked. Seabass bones make a particularly rich stock.

Several other distinct species are likely to be marketed under this name and are treated separately (see grouper and striped bass). They are relatively close in cooking characteristics, and are generally interchangeable in recipes.

Seabass with Oyster Sauce

This is an adaptation of a New Orleans recipe for redfish.

Alternatives: *Striped bass, corbina, Pacific halibut,*   *Serves 4*
grouper (A,G,P), snapper (A,G),
redfish (A,G)

2 teaspoons chopped garlic

4 scallions, white and pale
green parts, chopped

½ stalk celery, thinly sliced

4 tablespoons butter

¼ cup dry white wine

½ pint oysters with their
liquor

½ cup cream or *Crème
Fraiche (page 39)*

1½–2 pounds seabass filet

1 tablespoon chopped parsley

Salt and pepper to taste

Preheat the broiler.

In a skillet or heavy saucepan, sauté the garlic, scallions and celery in butter until softened but not browned. Add the wine, turn up the heat and reduce liquid by half. Add the cream and oyster liquor, reduce a little more and set aside while the fish is cooking.

Broil the fish on a buttered heatproof platter or roasting pan. Drain any liquid from the platter into the sauce. Add the oysters and parsley to the saucepan, and heat quickly until the oysters begin to curl. Pour the sauce over the fish and serve.

This sauce is suitable for grilled fish as well. Cut the filet into individual serving pieces, grill and serve in the same manner.

SHARK

Thresher Shark

(Alopias vulpinus)

Description: *Dark grey. Mottled below the lateral line. White belly.*	**Season:** *All year.*
	Fat Content: *Low.*
Size: *100 pounds typical.*	**Yield:** *80–90% boneless meat from blocks.*
Range: *Worldwide in temperate waters.*	**Available Forms:** *Steak, block.*

Leopard Shark
(Triakis semifasciata)

Description: *Light grey with black bars and spots.*	**Fat Content:** *Low.*
Size: *4–15 pounds.*	**Yield:** *20% filet or skinless steaks.*
Range: *Central Mexico to Oregon.*	**Available Forms:** *Round, filet, steak.*
Season: *All year.*	

Soupfin Shark
(Galeorhinus zyopterus)

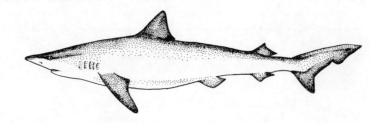

Description: *Dark grey fading to white. Black edges on front of dorsal and pectoral fins.*	**Season:** *All year.*
	Fat Content: *Low.*
Size: *30–50 pounds.*	**Yield:** *80% steak from block.*
Range: *Temperate waters of the Pacific.*	**Available Forms:** *Steak, filet.*

Until very recently, shark was an underrated and underutilized food fish. Most of the catch was processed for specialized purposes such as shark liver oil or dried fin for soup. The remaining meat was difficult to sell, and was frequently presented under pseudonyms or simply discarded at sea. In recent years, however, the public has accepted shark on its own terms. It is no longer the bargain it was a few years ago, but it is still reasonably priced.

Thresher shark, which gets its name from its extremely long, flail-like tail, is the most desirable shark widely available in the West. Leopard shark is the most common variety in in-shore waters and bays of California, and is often caught by fishermen fishing for other species. There is not much commercial exploitation of this species, despite its fine cooking qualities. The soupfin shark is highly prized for Chinese shark's fin soup, the rest of the fish being marketed separately.

In the East, mako shark is considered a close second to swordfish, and spiny dogfish is frequently served in fish and chips. Other commercial species include blue, brown and hammerhead sharks.

All sharks, because of their unique metabolism, tend to develop an aroma of ammonia. This can be neutralized by soaking the meat in a mild solution of vinegar or lemon juice, or in milk. The tough skin should always be removed, as it shrinks considerably in cooking, distorting the meat. Small sharks, such as the leopard, are easily fileted, but the larger varieties are generally used as steaks.

The very firm meat of shark has a mild to moderate flavor and very little fat; to prevent drying out in grilling or broiling, use an oil-based marinade or baste with a compound butter (pages 254–55) during cooking. Shark is a nice addition to fish soups and stews, and cold poached shark may be used like tuna in salads.

Alternatives: *Shark, swordfish and Pacific halibut steaks may be used interchangeably.*

Shark with Pesto

Alternatives: *Swordfish, halibut*   *Yield: 9-inch pie (6–10 servings)*

*1–1½ pounds shark filets
  or pieces*

Salt and pepper to taste

1 tablespoon oil

*2 tomatoes, peeled, seeded
  and coarsely chopped*

½ cup Pesto (see below)

Fresh basil leaves

Sauté the shark and tomatoes in oil. Turn the fish when it is half cooked. When done, remove from heat, add the pesto and toss the shark so it is evenly coated with the sauce. Garnish with basil leaves.

Pesto

Yield: About ½ cup

1 cup basil leaves

*2 tablespoons grated
  Parmesan cheese*

*2 tablespoons chopped pine
  nuts or walnuts*

2–4 cloves garlic, chopped

¼ cup or more olive oil

Combine the basil, Parmesan, nuts and garlic in a mortar, blender or food processor. Slowly add enough olive oil to produce a thick paste.

Shark Pie

This attractive dish makes a wonderful appetizer or main course.

Alternatives: *Swordfish,   Yield: 9-inch pie (6–10 servings)*
halibut

Crust

6 tablespoons cold butter

2 tablespoons olive oil

2 cups unbleached flour

6 tablespoons ice water

1 teaspoon grated lemon zest

Filling

1 pound boneless shark, cut into 1-inch cubes

1 pound fresh tomatoes, peeled, seeded and chopped or 2 cups canned tomatoes, drained and chopped

2-4 tablespoons chopped garlic

¼ cup green olives, pitted and sliced

2 tablespoons chopped parsley

2 teaspoons chopped capers

1 teaspoon fresh thyme or oregano, or ¼ teaspoon dried

Pepper to taste

Cut the butter and oil into the flour in a food processor or by hand. Add the ice water a little at a time, along with the lemon zest. Form the dough into a ball and refrigerate for at least 30 minutes and preferably 1 hour.

Preheat the oven to 400°.

Cut the dough in half. Flour a cutting board and a rolling pin. Roll out the dough from the center until it is about 3 inches larger than the diameter of the pie tin. Carefully place the pie crust into the tin and press it firmly in place. Cut off the excess.

S

A COOK'S ENCYCLOPEDIA OF SEAFOOD

204

Bake for 5 minutes or until the crust just begins to color. Remove from the oven and allow to cool slightly.

Roll out the other piece of dough to a slightly smaller diameter. Fill the pie with alternating layers of shark and tomatoes mixed with the capers, olives, parsley and garlic. Cover the pie with the top crust, pinching the two layers together at the outer edge. Lower the oven heat to 350°. Bake for 45 minutes or until the top crust turns golden brown. Serve hot or warm.

SHRIMP AND PRAWN

Spot Shrimp
(Pandalus platyceros)

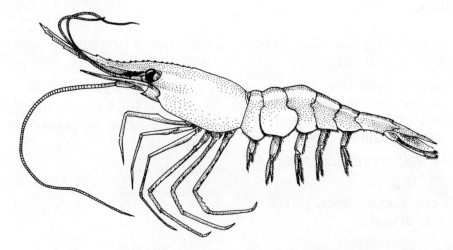

Other Names: *Monterey prawn, spot prawn.*	**Range:** *California coast, especially Monterey Bay.*
Description: *Pinkish red. Often with bright red roe attached.*	**Season:** *Spring–fall.*
	Fat Content: *Low.*
Size: *5–20 per pound.*	**Available Forms:** *Whole or with heads removed.*

Grass Shrimp
(Hippolyte californiensis)

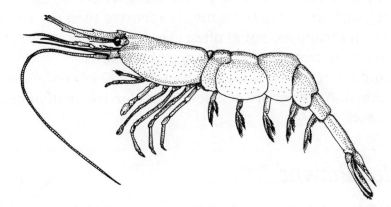

Description: *Translucent greyish-green.*	**Season:** *All year.*
Size: *150 per pound.*	**Fat Content:** *Low.*
Range: *Pacific coast.*	**Available Forms:** *Live, whole.*

The terms "shrimp" and "prawns" are used more or less inter-changeably in the West, with prawns generally referring to the larger sizes. We have followed this usage although, strictly speaking, prawns are a distinct and unrelated group of fresh-water crustaceans, including the aquacultured Malaysian prawn *(Macabrachium rosenbergii)*. Most of the shrimp available around the country are from the Gulf of Mexico and the waters of Baja California, and include several species of the family *Penaeidae*. The differences are of more interest to taxonomists than cooks, however.

Many cookbooks insist that shrimp should be deveined (the "vein" is in fact part of the digestive system extending through the tail). Others ridicule this practice as unnecessarily fastid-ious and a lot of trouble. Except where noted, we leave the choice up to the reader. The tiny grass shrimp can be cooked and eaten whole, although you may wish to remove the heads of the largest ones.

Shrimp tails are classified by size, according to the number of shrimp per pound. The largest sizes are preferred by most restaurants, and are likely to be more expensive than the smaller ones. Fresh shrimp are not as often classified by size as packaged tails, and may contain a wide range of sizes.

Shrimp are versatile; most varieties may be cooked by almost any method. All types are delicious grilled in the shell or peeled and sautéed.

Grilled Prawns

Grilling prawns in the shell always brings up the question of how to eat them. Shrimp and the smaller prawns can be eaten whole, shell and all, but the larger varieties must be peeled. Because they have to be eaten with the fingers, grilled prawns are most suited to backyard barbecues or other informal get-togethers.

Skewer the prawns through the tails with or without heads. After skewering, they can be marinated in olive oil mixed with fresh or dried herbs such as oregano, marjoram, thyme or rosemary, chopped garlic, salt and pepper.

Grill prawns over a hot fire, basting with the marinade. Large prawns will take 6–8 minutes to cook; they are done when the thick end of the tail is just turning opaque. Serve with Lemon-Garlic Butter (page 255), Fresh Tomato Salsa (page 262) or leftover *salsa* heated in butter.

Monterey Prawns with Green Tagliarini

The beautiful Monterey spot shrimp with their bright red roe are perfect for this dish. If these extra-large shellfish are not available, any other large shrimp or even crayfish tails will do.

Serves 4

1½–2 pounds whole prawns, including roe

¼ pound butter or Shrimp Butter (see below)

1 teaspoon chopped garlic

½ teaspoon fresh herbs, such as thyme, chervil or chives

1 cup cream or Crème Fraîche (page 39) at room temperature

1 pound fresh or dried spinach tagliarini or linguine

Salt and pepper to taste

Peel the prawns, reserving the heads and shells for Shrimp Butter. Set aside the roe, if any.

Heat the butter in a skillet; add the prawns, garlic and herbs. Sauté slowly, without browning the butter or garlic, until the prawns are nearly cooked. Meanwhile, cook the pasta. When the pasta is nearly ready, add the cream and roe to the skillet, turn the heat to high and reduce by one-third. Season to taste with salt and pepper, drain the pasta and toss it in the skillet until it is well coated with the sauce. Serve immediately on warmed plates, arranging the prawns and the roe on top of the pasta. (Note: If using dried pasta, reduce the sauce further, as the pasta will not absorb as much sauce.)

Shrimp Butter

Yield: ¼ cup

Heads and shells from 1½–2 pounds shrimp

¼ cup butter

Roughly chop the heads and shells with a knife or in a food processor. Place them in the top of a double boiler with the butter. Cook for at least 30 minutes, regulating the heat so that the butter does not boil. Strain the butter and discard the heads and shells. Refrigerate until ready to use, discarding any liquid which separates from the butter.

Shrimp butter freezes well, so it can be made any time you have shells; or, you can freeze shells until you accumulate enough to make a large batch. Crab, crayfish or lobster shells can be used in the same manner.

Kung Pao Shrimp
Bruce Cost

Alternatives: *Squid rings* *Serves 6 or more as a side dish*
Serves 4 as a main course

1 pound shrimp (20–24 per pound) shelled and deveined or grass shrimp

1 tablespoon cornstarch

¼ cup red wine vinegar

Salt to taste

2 tablespoons light soy sauce

5 teaspoons sugar

1 cup oil

6–12 dried hot red peppers

1½ tablespoons peeled and chopped fresh ginger root

4–6 cloves garlic, chopped

2–3 tablespoons chopped scallions

Rinse and dry the shrimp. Dust them with cornstarch and set aside. Combine the vinegar, salt, soy sauce and sugar. Set aside.

In a wok or large skillet, heat the oil until hot. Add the shrimp and stir-fry until done, about 1½ minutes. Drain in a sieve or colander, pouring off all but 1½ tablespoons of oil. Fry the dried peppers until black in remaining oil. Add the ginger, garlic and scallions, then the vinegar mixture. Bring to a boil and add the shrimp, stirring until they are well coated and hot. Serve with rice.

Shrimp Tempura

Bruce Cost

Serves 3–4 as a main course

1 pound shrimp (20–24 per pound or larger), shelled and deveined

2 teaspoons salt

2 teaspoons baking soda

Oil for frying

Slice the shrimp almost all the way through the back and flatten. Mix the shrimp with salt and baking soda. Let stand for 30 minutes or so.

Dipping Sauce

1 tablespoon oil

1 tablespoon minced ginger

1 tablespoon tomato paste

2 tablespoons sugar

3 tablespoons white vinegar

1 tablespoon light soy sauce

½ teaspoon salt

1 cup water

1½ tablespoons cornstarch dissolved in ¼ cup water

2 teaspoons chili oil (available in Asian groceries)

In a saucepan, cook the ginger and tomato paste in oil until the oil is well colored. Stir in the sugar, vinegar, soy sauce, salt and water and bring to a boil. Add the cornstarch mixture and simmer until thickened and clear. Stir in the chili oil.

Batter

1 cup flour

½ teaspoon salt

2 teaspoons baking powder

1 cup water

Combine the flour, salt and baking soda. Stir in the water,

but don't overmix. The batter may be slightly lumpy. Rinse off the salt and soda from the shrimp under cold water and drain well.

Heat the oil to almost smoking (375°). Dip the shrimp in the batter and fry until golden brown. Drain on paper towels and serve with the sauce.

Tempura is traditionally made with vegetables as well as shrimp. Most commonly used are thin-sliced sweet potato, carrot, green beans and zucchini or other summer squash.

Sautéed Shrimp

This recipe is adaptable to any kind of prawn or shrimp.

Serves 2

1 pound whole shrimp or
  prawns

3 tablespoons oil

1 teaspoon chopped garlic

¼ cup dry white wine

1 teaspoon chopped herbs
  such as parsley or thyme

1 tablespoon softened butter
  (optional)

1 pound tomatoes, peeled,
  seeded and roughly chopped

Salt and pepper to taste

Remove heads and shells from the shrimp, reserving them for
Shrimp Butter (page 207). Devein if desired. Heat the oil in a
skillet. Add the shrimp and cook until the meat is opaque.
Remove the shrimp to a warm plate. Pour out all but 1 tablespoon of the oil. Add the garlic, white wine and fresh herbs.
Reduce the liquid by half. Add the butter. Toss the tomatoes in
the sauce until they are warmed. Return the shrimp to the pan
momentarily to heat through.

Arrange the shrimp, tails pointed out, in a circle on individual
plates. Place the tomatoes in the center. Pour the sauce over
the shrimp.

SKATE

(Raja inornata)

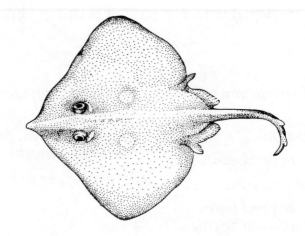

Other Names: *Ray, raja.*	**Season:** *All year.*
Description: *Olive above, tan below.*	**Fat Content:** *Low.*
Size: *1–5 pounds (wings).*	**Yield:** *50% filet from whole wings, 65% from skinless.*
Range: *California to Alaska.*	**Available Forms:** *Wings, skinned wings.*

Like shark, skate wings should be soaked in acidulated water or cooked in an acid liquid such as Court-Bouillon (page 251). It is possible to grill them, but they are more commonly poached, sautéed or served cold as in Angler Salad (page 59). Poached skate is typically served with Brown Butter (page 255). Kimberly Mowers of Monterey Fish in Berkeley suggests rolling skate wing filets around a bread crumb and vegetable stuffing and baking them sealed in foil. The cooking juices can then be enriched with butter to form a sauce.

SMELT

(Allosmerus elongatus)

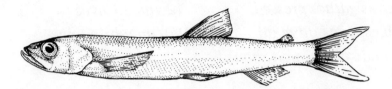

<table>
<tr><td>Other Names: Whitebait.</td><td>Season: Spring–fall.</td></tr>
</table>

Other Names: *Whitebait.*

Description: *Greenish gold dorsally. Silver sides.*

Size: *3–7 inches.*

Range: *California to Washington.*

Season: *Spring–fall.*

Fat Content: *Moderate.*

Available Forms: *Round.*

Similar Species: *Surf smelt* (Hypomesus pretiosus).

These tiny fish are frequently eaten whole; they may, however, be pan-dressed if desired. They are best lightly floured and pan-fried or deep-fried, and served with a lemon wedge. Larger fish may be used in recipes for herring or fresh anchovies.

Smelt Baked in Grape Leaves

Alternatives: *Anchovies*   *Serves 6 as an appetizer*

6 cloves garlic, pressed

2 tablespoons olive oil

1 pound small smelt, boned

12 grape leaves

¼ cup white wine

Preheat the oven to 350°.

Combine the garlic and olive oil. Place 2 or 3 smelt at the bottom of a leaf and spread with a little of the oil-garlic mixture. Roll the leaf around the fish, forming an envelope. Place rolls seam side down in a small oiled baking dish. Moisten with the wine. Bake for 35–40 minutes. Serve hot or warm.

SOLE

Petrale

(Eopsetta jordani)

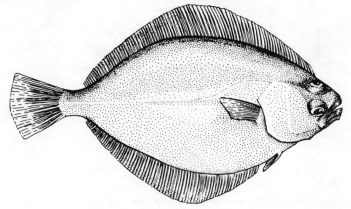

Other Names: *Petrale sole, brill.*	**Season:** *All year. Most common in winter.*
Description: *Uniform olive green to dark brown above.*	**Fat Content:** *Low.*
Size: *1–5 pounds.*	**Yield:** *35% filet.*
Range: *Central California to Alaska.*	**Available Forms:** *Round, filet.*

Rex Sole
(Glyptocephalus zachirus)

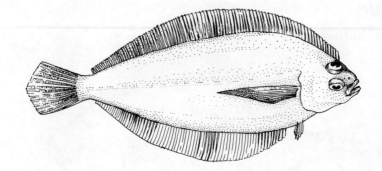

Description: *Medium brown above, variable color below.*	**Season:** *All year.*
	Fat Content: *Low.*
Size: *To 1 pound.*	**Yield:** *35% filet.*
Range: *Central California to Alaska.*	**Available Forms:** *Round, pan-dressed.*

English Sole
(Parophrys vetulus)

Description: *Olive green to light brown above.*	**Season:** *All year.*
	Fat Content: *Low.*
Size: *½–2 pounds.*	**Yield:** *20–30% filet.*
Range: *Pacific coast. Mainly Monterey to British Columbia.*	**Available Forms:** *Filet, only occasionally round.*

As European food writers are quick to point out, the many species of North American flatfish known as "sole" are not true soles, but flounders. Semantic quibbles aside, the name encompasses some of our most delicious and valuable species as well as some of our most undistinguished.

Petrale is the favorite among Pacific soles, and the finest in flavor and texture. It is mostly marketed in filet form, but is worth seeking out round as well. Rex sole is a close second, and is actually preferred by some. It is almost never available in filet form. While these two species are generally found under their own names, any fish labeled "filet of sole" without any further information is most likely English sole, a plentiful species of average to good quality.

The color of the skin on the underside of soles, especially rex and petrale, varies according to the bottom surface of the ocean where they are caught. Generally, the whiter the skin the better the texture and flavor of the flesh.

Classic French cuisine has built up a whole repertoire of fish preparations, from *à l'américaine* to Walewska, around the delicate flavor and texture of sole filets. Most of these involve poaching or sautéing; however, with practice and careful timing, they may be grilled with excellent results. Pan-dressed rex sole (and smaller petrale) are more easily grilled, or may be baked in batter.

Alternatives: *Filets of any species of flounder or John Dory may be substituted for sole.*

Filet of Sole Meunière

Serves 4

1½ pounds sole filets

Salt and pepper to taste

All-purpose flour

4 tablespoons butter

1 cup assorted vegetables, julienned and blanched, such as carrots, zucchini, leeks, celery root, summer squash

Juice of 1 lemon

1 tablespoon chopped parsley for garnish

Season the filets with salt and pepper and dredge them in flour. Sauté the fish over medium heat in 2 tablespoons of the butter until golden brown on both sides. (Thinner filets require higher heat to brown the coating without overcooking the flesh, while thicker filets must cook somewhat slower.) While the filets cook, sauté the vegetables in the remaining butter. Transfer the fish to warmed plates; deglaze the pan with lemon juice and pour over the fish. Garnish with the vegetables and top with chopped parsley.

Filet of Sole Florentine

In classic French cooking, "Florentine" denotes dishes prepared with spinach. Ours is a simple version of this dish. Shrimp Butter is a nice touch, but not essential.

Serves 4

¾ pound spinach, washed, with stems removed

2 tablespoons butter or Shrimp Butter (page 207)

1 tablespoon chopped shallots

½ teaspoon paprika

3–4 cups Fumet (page 252)

¼ pound cooked shrimp or ¼ pound mushrooms, sliced and sautéed (optional)

½ cup cream

1½ pounds sole filets

In a covered saucepan, cook the spinach in just the water clinging to the leaves. Toss with a little butter if desired, and keep warm. Sauté the shallots and paprika in butter or Shrimp Butter. When they are nearly cooked, add ½ cup of *fumet*, the shrimp or mushrooms and the cream. Reduce by half and correct the seasoning. Meanwhile, poach the filets in *fumet*. Arrange them on a bed of spinach and cover with the sauce.

Filet of Sole Stuffed with Shrimp

Almost any kind of shellfish, including crab, scallops or even lobster, can be substituted for the shrimp. Handling the stuffed filets is not as tricky as it seems. Any excess stuffing or bits of stuffing that fall out of the rolled filets can be incorporated into the sauce.

Serves 4

2 tablespoons butter

2 cloves garlic, chopped

½ cup finely diced yellow onion

6–8 ounces cooked small shrimp

¼ cup chopped parsley

2–3 cups Fumet (page 252), heated

8 small sole filets (2–3 ounces each)

½ cup cream

Sauté the garlic and onion in 1 tablespoon of butter until soft; allow to cool. Combine all but 1 tablespoon of the shrimp with the parsley and the cooled onion and garlic. Divide the stuffing in eighths and roll each of the filets around the stuffing, allowing at least an inch of overlap.

Place the filets, seam side down, in a buttered or oiled pan just large enough to hold them and at least 3 inches deep. Pour the hot *fumet* into the pan, being careful not to wash the stuffing out of the rolled filets. Poach at a simmer until filets are just done.

Carefully remove filets to a warm serving dish or individual plates. Pour out all but ¼ cup of the *fumet*. Add the cream and the reserved shrimp and reduce. Correct the seasoning and pour the sauce over the filets.

Filet of Sole Stuffed with Mushrooms

This is prepared exactly as the previous recipe, but with a *duxelles* mixture replacing the shrimp stuffing.

Serves 4

2–3 cups Fumet (page 252),   ½ cup cream
   heated
8 small sole filets (2–3
   ounces each)

Duxelles
(Mushroom and Bread Crumb Stuffing)

2 tablespoons butter   ¼ cup bread crumbs
½ cup chopped mushrooms   2 tablespoons chopped
3–4 cloves garlic, chopped   parsley
½ cup finely diced yellow   Juice of ½ lemon
   onion   Salt and pepper to taste

Sauté the mushrooms, garlic and onion in butter until most of the liquid released by the mushrooms is evaporated. Add the bread crumbs and parsley, lemon juice and salt and pepper. Allow to cool before stuffing filets as described in previous recipe.

SPOTTED SEA TROUT

(Cynoscion nebulosus)

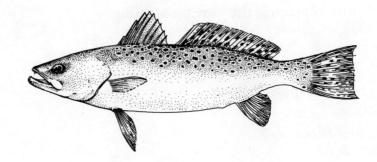

Other Names: *Speckled trout, sea trout, weakfish.*	**Season:** *All year. Especially spring and fall.*
Description: *Dark grey fading to silver. Black spots on upper body and fins.*	**Fat Content:** *Moderate.*
	Yield: *33% filet.*
Size: *1–5 pounds.*	**Available Forms:** *Round, dressed, pan-dressed.*
Range: *Atlantic and Gulf coasts.*	

Like redfish, this Atlantic croaker is becoming increasingly available on the West Coast. See seabass and corbina for recipes.

SQUID

(Loligo opalescens)

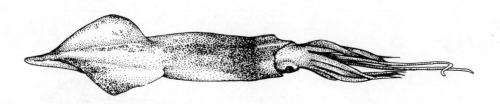

Other Names: *Market squid, common squid, calamari.*	**Season:** *April–October in northern California. December–April in southern California.*
Description: *Ivory skin with tiny purple to brown dots.*	**Fat Content:** *Low.*
Size: *4–10 per pound.*	**Yield:** *67% meat, including tentacles.*
Range: *Pacific coast from Southern California to Washington.*	**Available Forms:** *Fresh, fresh cleaned, frozen whole, frozen cleaned.*

This abundant and delicious mollusc has until recently been relegated to the bait box because of its odd appearance or because it is often overcooked and tough. It is becoming extremely popular because it is inexpensive and versatile.

Squid can be poached and used in salads, sautéed, fried, stuffed and baked, braised or grilled. Japanese species are eaten raw. For more information on squid, see *The International Squid Cookbook* by Isaac Cronin (Aris Books, 1981).

Cleaning Squid

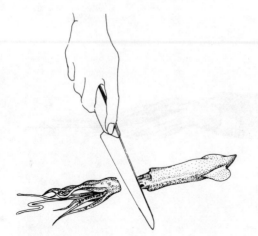

1 Cut off the tentacles just above the eye. Save them.

2 Squeeze out the beak, the squid's mouth, which looks like a garbanzo bean. Discard it.

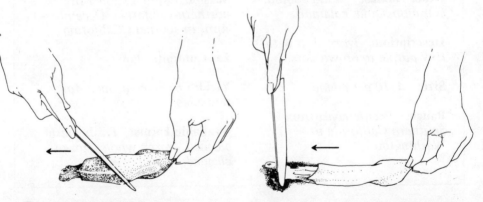

3 Holding the blade of a chef's knife almost flat, scrape along the body from the tail to the opening. Press down hard to squeeze out the entrails, but be careful not to break the skin. Don't worry about removing the skin, which is edible.

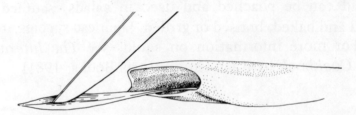

4 With the point of the knife, stab the transparent quill which protrudes from the body and hold it fast. Pull the body away. The quill should remain under the knife. Discard the quill. The squid is now ready for stuffing. If you want to cook smaller pieces, cut rings crosswise ½–1 inch wide.

Squid Stuffed with Spinach

Serves 4

2 pounds large squid, cleaned
    for stuffing

2 tablespoons olive oil

1 medium yellow onion,
    chopped

½ pound spinach, washed,
    drained, stems removed
    and leaves chopped

¼ cup bread crumbs

1½ ounces Pernod or other
    anise liqueur

Salt and pepper to taste

2 tablespoons olive oil

1 cup cream

Chop the tentacles and set aside.

Sauté the onions in olive oil until soft. Add the spinach and cook until wilted. Add the tentacles and bread crumbs. Sauté for 2 minutes. Add half the Pernod and remove from the heat. (It is best to let the stuffing cool to room temperature before adding it to the squid. If this is impossible, make the stuffing and stuff the squid immediately before cooking.) Stuff the squid loosely with the spinach mixture, using a pastry bag, small spoon or your fingers. Seal each with a toothpick.

Heat 2 tablespoons of olive oil in a skillet large enough to hold all the squid in one layer. Add the squid and sauté until the bodies are opaque, about 4 minutes. Remove to a heated serving dish. Deglaze the pan with the remaining Pernod. Add the cream, turn up the heat, and reduce by two-thirds. Return the squid to the skillet to reheat.

Arrange the squid on a warm platter, removing the tooth-picks in the kitchen if desired. Pour the sauce over and serve.

Squid with Black Rice

Serves 4

2 pounds squid, cleaned,
  bodies cut into rings,
  with tentacles
  and ink sacs reserved

2 tablespoons olive oil

¼ cup chopped yellow onion

1 tablespoon chopped garlic

1 cup white rice

1 teaspoon fresh thyme or
  oregano, or ¼ teaspoon
  dried

1 bay leaf

Salt to taste

1 cup chicken stock and 1
  cup water (if using
  canned chicken broth,
  decrease salt)

In a sieve placed over a bowl, crush the ink sacs with the back of a spoon. Pour the stock and water through the sieve to extract the rest of the ink.

In a medium-sized casserole, sauté the onion and garlic in the olive oil over medium heat; do not brown. Add the rice, stir and sauté a few minutes longer until the rice just begins to color. Add the seasonings and the stock. Cover, bring to a boil, reduce heat and simmer for 15 minutes or until most of the liquid has been absorbed. Taste for seasoning. Add the squid and cook 5 minutes more or until squid is opaque and rice has absorbed the remaining liquid.

Serve from the casserole or transfer to a serving dish, arranging the squid on top. Serve with an assortment of colorful vegetables.

Mexican Squid Salad

Calamares en Escabeche

Serves 4 as an appetizer

1 pound squid, cleaned, bodies cut into rings, with tentacles

1 tablespoon lemon or lime juice

1 teaspoon red wine vinegar

4 tablespoons olive oil

2 or more serrano or other fresh chiles, seeded and chopped

¼ cup chopped cilantro

1 medium tomato, seeded and cut into ¼-inch dice

2 tablespoons sliced scallion tops or diced red onion

Salt to taste

In a large saucepan or pasta pot with removable strainer, boil the squid in abundant salted water just until opaque, a minute or less. Drain and rinse immediately with cold water to prevent overcooking.

Combine the remaining ingredients in a bowl. Toss the squid in the dressing and marinate, refrigerated, for 1–4 hours. Correct seasoning. Serve on a bed of lettuce.

Squid with Salted Mustard Greens

Salted mustard greens are a common accompaniment for seafood and pork dishes in southern China. When the greens are boiled, they produce a rich broth which is the basis for soups and sauces.

Serves 4 or more as a side dish   *Serves 2 as a main course*

¼ *pound salted mustard*
greens (available in Asian
groceries)

2 *tablespoons oil*

1 *tablespoon chopped fresh*
ginger

1 *tablespoon chopped garlic*

1 *pound squid, cleaned and*
cut into rings

1 *teaspoon soy sauce*

1 *teaspoon cornstarch*
dissolved in 1 tablespoon
water

Cover the mustard greens with water and simmer slowly for 45–60 minutes. Strain, reserving ½ cup of the liquid. Cut the mustard greens into ¼-inch slices. In a heavy skillet or wok, sauté the ginger and garlic in oil until almost cooked. Add the squid and sauté 30 seconds. Add the mustard greens, broth and soy sauce. Cook 2 minutes over highest heat. Add the cornstarch mixture. When the sauce thickens, remove from the heat and serve immediately.

Squid Stuffing for Pasta

Squid, after it is briefly blanched, can be made into a paste not that different from a meatball mixture. It can be formed into balls and sautéed or used as a stuffing for ravioli, tortellini or other stuffed pasta. Squid balls may also be braised in olive oil and chicken stock.

Yield: Enough filling for about 24 ravioli or 12 squid balls

1 pound squid, including
   tentacles, cleaned and
   cut into pieces
2 tablespoons grated
   Parmesan cheese

2 cloves garlic, chopped
1 tablespoon chopped parsley
1 egg yolk
¼ cup bread crumbs

Blanch the squid in boiling water for 10 seconds. Stop the cooking by rinsing the squid in cold water. Combine the squid and the rest of the ingredients in a blender or food processor. The mixture should form a very thick paste. Add more bread crumbs if necessary. Use immediately or refrigerate for up to 4 hours.

STRIPED BASS

(Morone saxatilis)

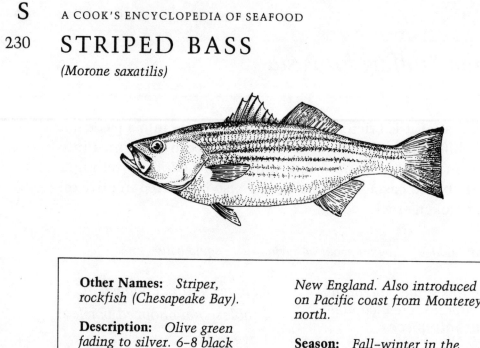

Other Names: *Striper, rockfish (Chesapeake Bay).*	*New England. Also introduced on Pacific coast from Monterey north.*
Description: *Olive green fading to silver. 6–8 black longitudinal stripes. Large, heavy scales.*	**Season:** *Fall–winter in the East. Early winter–spring in the West.*
Size: *To 50 pounds. 2–15 pounds typical.*	**Fat Content:** *Moderate.*
Range: *Atlantic coast from Chesapeake Bay to southern*	**Yield:** *40% filet, 65% steak.*

On the West Coast, only anglers and their families and friends get to taste this delicious fish, as it is an introduced game species. Its flesh is firm and moderately sweet. Like other anadromous (freshwater-breeding) saltwater fish, it is susceptible to parasites and should not be eaten raw. Grilling, broiling, poaching and steaming are all appropriate cooking methods. For recipes, see corbina and seabass.

STEELHEAD

(Salmo gairdneri)

This is the common name for the migratory form of rainbow trout. The flesh of fish caught on their return to fresh water resembles salmon in color and flavor due to their oceanic diet. Although steelhead is a game fish in California, it is brought into our markets from the Columbia River. It may be cooked in any way appropriate to salmon. (See trout for a description of this fish.)

WHITE STURGEON

(Acipenser transmontanus)

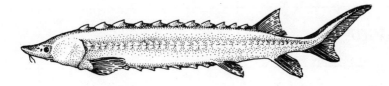

Description: *Uniform pale grey. Bony plates along back and sides.*	**Fat Content:** *High.*
	Yield: *50% steaks.*
Size: *10–1000 pounds and up.*	**Available Forms:** *Block, steak, filet.*
Range: *Ocean, bays, major rivers from Monterey north to southern Alaska.*	**Similar Species:** *Green sturgeon (A. medirostris) is a smaller, fattier species which is generally smoked; it is less desirable fresh.*
Season: *Winter–spring.*	

A sportfish in California, sturgeon is harvested commercially in the Columbia River, and is available here both fresh and smoked. The protected population in the Sacramento River system is slowly recovering from being overfished almost to the point of extinction. (Early in this century, California's caviar production was second only to the Russian and Iranian enterprises in the Caspian and Black seas.) With careful management, the California population may again support a commercial fishery.

Sturgeon's dense rich flesh varies somewhat in flavor. At best it is clean and sweet, but it may at times have a pronounced freshwater flavor. Check the aroma of any piece in question, and avoid those with a muddy smell. Like shark, sturgeon should be skinned, or the shrinking skin will produce misshapen steaks. Perhaps the best form for grilling or sautéing is thin diagonal slices or scallops, up to ½ inch thick. Marinate in olive oil and strong herbs and serve with an herb or brown butter.

Caviar

Tom Worthington, a young Bay Area chef, provided this recipe.

In the strictest sense, caviar is the salted roe of sturgeon. In Europe, only sturgeon roe may be sold as caviar, while in the United States similarly treated salmon roe is sold as "red caviar." Several other species produce roe which is commercially processed into "caviar," including Icelandic lumpfish and Great Lakes whitefish; these must, however, carry the name of the fish on the label.

Making caviar is a relatively simple process. Its success depends upon the condition of the roe as well as upon thorough cleaning and careful handling. The following recipe may be used for any edible roe if sturgeon or salmon roe are unavailable. (Caution: Do not use roes of cabezon or alligator gar, which are toxic.)

Choosing the Roe

Test the tenderness of the roe by crushing one egg between your fingers. The roe is good to use for caviar if the egg offers no resistance as you pop it. Roe which is too firm makes tough caviar.

Test the roe for flavor by breaking one raw egg with your tongue against the roof of your mouth. Here too, the egg should offer no resistance. It should taste fresh, not fishy, and should leave no aftertaste.

Separating the Roe

Cut the egg sac in half. Make a cut along the length of each of the two pieces. Cut just deep enough to pierce the outer membrane. Open the egg sac flat on a board and, with a knife, scrape the eggs away from the membrane into a glass or stainless steel bowl.

Cleaning the Roe

Place the loose eggs in a fine-meshed sieve. Gently pour several batches of cold water over the roe until the water that drains through is perfectly clear.

Curing the Roe

Carefully cover the roe with a lukewarm 7% brine solution (2.24 ounces salt per quart of water). Let the roe sit in the brine solution for 15 minutes, or until the eggs have reached the desired saltiness (test by tasting a few eggs).

Aging the Caviar

Pack the caviar in jars. Store, refrigerated, for at least a week before serving. (This aging improves the flavor; the caviar is, however, perfectly edible right after salting.) Keep refrigerated until ready to serve, and use within a month after packing.

SWORDFISH

(Xiphias gladius)

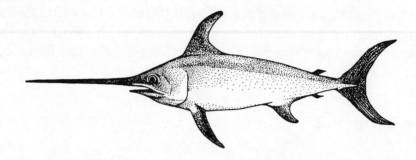

Description: *Dark grey above. Yellowish below.*	**Season:** *All year.*
Size: *100–200 pounds typical.*	**Fat Content:** *Moderate.*
	Yield: *80% meat from block.*
Range: *Worldwide in temperate and tropical oceans.*	**Available Forms:** *Block, steak.*

Among sportfishermen, swordfish is one of the most popular of the billed fishes, and has the best eating qualities. It gets its name from its long, flattened bill with which it slashes and impales its prey. It has been known to attack boats and other floating objects.

Until recently, swordfish were taken mainly by harpoon as they sunned themselves near the surface. Recent developments in fishing methods, including long-line angling and gill netting, and the discovery of the wintering grounds, have resulted in swordfish being available all year.

The firm, dense, fine flesh of swordfish is the most meatlike in texture of all fish, and one of the most popular. It is a universal favorite for grilling and broiling, and takes well to sauces with such pronounced flavors as anchovy, rosemary, garlic and mustard. However, this fish is much in demand and tends to be expensive.

For an inexpensive alternative, ask the fish dealer for a chunk from the base of the tail which should be available at a lower price. With a bit of carving, you can separate pieces of tender flesh from the whiter, sinewy portion. Cut these into ½–1-inch pieces for brochettes, or use in place of shark in Shark Pie (page 203).

Grilled Swordfish with Gin-Vermouth Beurre Blanc

Carol Brendlinger

Alternatives: *Salmon or steelhead steaks or filets*   *Serves 4*

⅓ cup mixed white wine vinegar and lemon juice

⅔ cup white vermouth

2 shallots, chopped

1 tablespoon gin

1½ teaspoons crushed juniper berries, roasted and coarsely ground

¼ cup butter

1–1½ pounds swordfish steaks

Combine the vinegar, lemon juice, vermouth and shallots in a saucepan and slowly reduce the liquid to a thick paste. Add the gin and ½ teaspoon of the juniper berries and combine. Whisk in the butter, an ounce at a time, over gentle heat.

Strain the sauce through a fine sieve, and keep it warm in a double boiler or water bath.

Dust one side of the swordfish with ½ teaspoon of the ground juniper. Place that side face down on the grill. When the fish is half cooked, dust the top side with juniper and turn. Serve the swordfish covered with sauce.

TILEFISH

(Lopholatilus chamaeleonticeps)

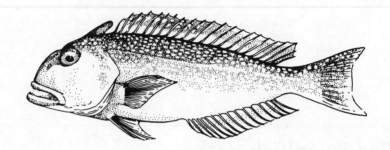

Other Names: *Tile bass.*	**Season:** *All year. Least common in summer.*
Description: *Sea green with yellow spots fading to cream.*	**Fat Content:** *Low.*
Size: *2–30 pounds.*	**Yield:** *40% filet.*
Range: *Atlantic and Gulf of Mexico.*	**Available Forms:** *Dressed, filet, steak, chunk.*

A common East Coast variety, tilefish serves the same need there as rockfish does on the West Coast: a plentiful, mild fish suitable to a variety of cooking methods. It is occasionally available here, and may be used in any rockfish recipe.

Tilefish Steamed in Spinach Leaves

In Southeast Asia, fish is often cooked in banana leaves. The result is moist and delicate. Spinach leaves are a good substitute as they impart a little water, and the entire package is delicious to eat.

Alternatives: *Rockfish, sablefish*

Serves 4 or more as a side dish
Serves 2 as a main course

½ *pound tilefish filet, cut into 1-ounce scallops or slices*

2 *stalks fresh lemongrass, cut in thirds, or 2 teaspoons dried lemongrass soaked in water for 30 minutes*

4 *thin slices of ginger*

¼ *cup oil*

6–8 *large spinach leaves, stems removed*

¼ *cup chicken stock*

1 *tablespoon fish sauce (page 40)*

Marinate the filets in the lemongrass, ginger and oil for 1–2 hours. Blanch or steam the spinach until wilted and set aside to cool.

Wrap each piece of fish with a spinach leaf. If you are using fresh lemongrass, put a piece in each package; if using dried lemongrass, discard it. Pour the chicken stock and fish sauce onto a plate in the top of a steamer. Bring the water to a boil. Add the spinach packages and steam until done, about 5 minutes. Remove the lemongrass stems and reseal the packages. Pour the sauce from the plate over the fish and serve.

RAINBOW TROUT

(Salmo gairdneri)

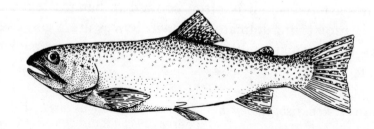

Other Names: *Steelhead (in ocean-run form).*

Description: *Olive green fading through rainbow hue along lateral line to silver. Irregular black spots.*

Size: *Typically 1–2 pounds in the wild, but up to 50 pounds. 8 ounces–1 pound when aquacultured.*

Range: *Western North American streams. Widely aquacultured throughout the United States, especially in the West.*

Season: *All year.*

Fat Content: *High.*

Yield: *67% from aquacultured fish.*

Available Forms: *Dressed, boned, smoked.*

Similar Species: *Other game species such as golden, brown, brook, Dolly Varden and cutthroat trouts are also prized as food fish.*

Probably the most familiar aquacultured fish in the United States, rainbow trout is widely available fresh. Its flesh is whiter and milder in flavor than that of wild trout. Most fish are marketed at exactly 8 ounces dressed weight, a concession no doubt to the needs of restaurants and hotels for portion control.

Dressed fish may be grilled, sautéed or poached in a Court-Bouillon (page 251). Boned fish may be stuffed with Oyster

Stuffing for Fish (page 166) or Bread Crumb Stuffing (page 133) and baked or flattened and sautéed *meunière* style. With its mild freshwater flavor, trout needs a sauce with assertive ingredients. Capers are a classic companion, and like all the salmonids, trout shows a particular affinity for dill.

Alternatives: *Pan-sized coho or king salmon.*

Smoked Fish Salad

Bruce Aidells of Poulet in Berkeley created this hearty fish and potato salad.

Alternatives: *Smoked whitefish*   *Serves 6 as a first course*

12 small new potatoes, peeled, boiled, sliced (or cubed) and chilled

1 small red onion, thinly sliced

1 pound boneless smoked trout, cut into small pieces

¼ cup oil and vinegar dressing

¼ cup Mayonnaise (page 257)

1 tablespoon chopped parsley

Fresh dill to taste

Lettuce

In a large bowl, toss all the ingredients until the potatoes and fish are well moistened. Serve each portion on a bed of lettuce.

TUNA

Albacore

(Thunnus alalunga)

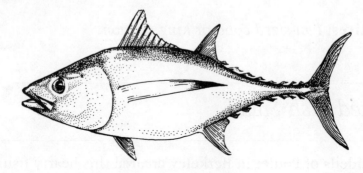

Description: *Steel grey or blue fading to lighter blue. Extremely long pectoral fin.*	**Season:** *Summer and early fall.*
Size: *To 40 pounds.*	**Fat Content:** *High.*
	Yield: *60% filet or steak.*
Range: *Tropical and temperate oceans of the world.*	**Available Forms:** *Dressed, filet, steak.*

Yellowfin Tuna

(T. albacares)

Description: *Similar to albacore but darker. Bright yellow in most fins.*	**Season:** *All year. Most plentiful in summer.*
Size: *To 300 pounds.*	**Similar Species:** *Bluefin tuna* (T. thynnus), *bigeye tuna* (T. obesus).

While albacore commands the highest price among canned tunas, it can be the least expensive fresh tuna during its short season. The other tuna species, with darker flesh and full flavor, are the types marketed in cans as "light" tuna. They are also the choice varieties for Sashimi (see below) and *sushi*.

All the tunas have fairly firm, distinctively rich-flavored flesh suitable to dry-heat cooking. To those who have only tasted tuna from a can, a fresh tuna steak grilled over charcoal and served with a Maître d'Hotel Butter (page 254) will be a pleasant surprise. The canned version will also pale in comparison to a salad made with freshly poached tuna (page 35). Tuna also makes a nice topping for pizza (page 269).

Alternatives: *Bonito, wahoo, spearfish.*

Sashimi

Christopher Lally

Sashimi is a Japanese style of eating raw fish and shellfish. It requires two things above all—fresh seafood and smooth, quick cutting with a sharp knife.

Sashimi cutting is traditionally done with a thin-bladed knife, although a chef's knife will do. To preserve the texture of the fish, the blade should be pulled rapidly through the flesh in an even motion. Sawing will tear the fish. All the *sashimi* cutting techniques we have included were demonstrated by Christopher Lally, Bay Area chef and cooking teacher.

Serve *sashimi* with a mixture of soy sauce and *wasabi* (page 44) to taste or with soy sauce and lemon juice.

Tuna Sashimi

The following cutting instructions are for a section of filet from the back (dorsal) side of a fairly small tuna. Step 1 shows the filet placed skin side down on the cutting board.

1 Pieces A,B and the two tri-
angles of C are generally
used for sashimi. The large
portion of C is cooked and
served with a sauce (see
below). The small end piece
of C is discarded.

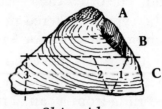

Skin side

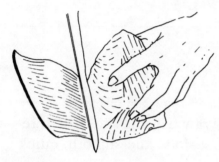

2 Skin the
filet.

3 Cut off the dark material
and discard it.

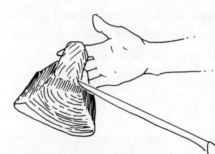

4 Cut off piece A, slicing
across ¾ inch from the
top. Cut a second piece B the
same width. Cut A across the
grain into ¾-inch-wide pieces.

5 Cut B in half with the grain. Cut both B pieces into ¾-inch-wide pieces.

6 Make two triangular-shaped pieces by cutting lengthwise along lines 1 and 2 on C (not illustrated).

Section C, which is not typically used for *sashimi*, can be trimmed and poached in a green tea-soy sauce mixture as follows:

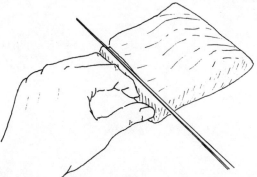

7 Trim and discard the tough fibrous end of section C by cutting along line 3.

8 Cut, with the grain, into ¾-inch slices. There should be 5 or 6 pieces. These pieces can be prepared in the following manner:

Poaching Liquid for Tuna

¼ cup green tea liquid   ½ tablespoon crushed ginger
1½ ounces soy sauce   1 tablespoon chopped scallion

Combine all the ingredients and poach tuna in the mixture for 3 minutes. Remove the tuna from the liquid and let it cool. Serve the fish with the poaching liquid as a sauce.

Squid Sashimi

One exception to the rule of fresh seafood for *sashimi* is squid. The Japanese make *sashimi* from their own large variety known as *mongo ika*. This species is usually available in this country in frozen chunks.

After thawing the squid, pull off the transparent membrane which covers the body.

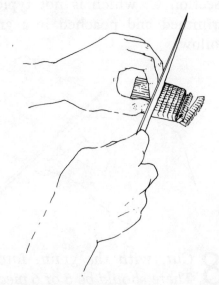

1 Make parallel lengthwise cuts ⅛ inch apart, slicing to within ⅛ inch of the other side.

2 Cut ³⁄₁₆-inch slices perpendicular to the first cuts.

3 Open up each slice into a half circle. Arrange the slices on a serving tray.

Mackerel Sashimi

Dress and filet a small mackerel, reserving the skeleton and head (pages 23–28).

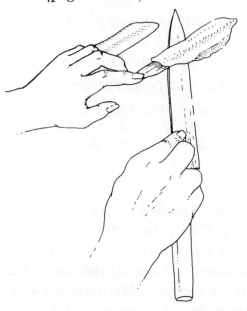 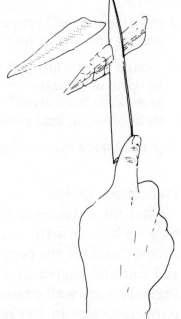

1 Skin the filets (page 25).

2 Cut the meat at a 45-degree angle into ¾-inch slices. You will get 5 or 6 slices per filet.

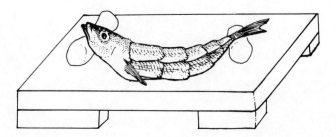

3 Prop the head and tail up with pieces of daikon (page 146), carrot or other vegetable. Arrange both filets on top of the bones, overlapped like fish scales.

Fresh Tuna Salad

Alternatives: *Halibut, shark, bonito*   *Serves 4 as an appetizer*

2 red or green bell peppers,
  seeded and cut in half

½ pound tuna filet, poached
  in wine or Fumet
  (page 252), marinated
  with olive oil and chilled

1–2 teaspoons chopped garlic

3 tablespoons or more
  olive oil

1–2 tablespoons lemon juice

Salt and pepper to taste

1 head butter or red leaf
  lettuce, washed and
  thoroughly dried

Preheat the broiler.

Char the outsides of the peppers. Remove the skins by rubbing each piece with a paper towel. Cut the peppers into thin slices. Combine the peppers, tuna, garlic, olive oil, lemon juice and salt and pepper in a small bowl. Toss until the tuna and vegetables are well coated with the dressing. Marinate at room temperature or in the refrigerator for 30 minutes to 2 hours. Serve the salad on a bed of lettuce.

This salad may also be dressed with a flavored mayonnaise (pages 257–59), thinned with oil and lemon juice.

WAHOO

(Acanthocybium solandri)

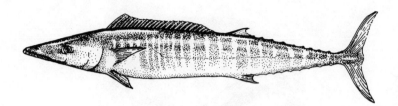

Other Names: *Ono.*	**Season:** *Winter–spring.*
Description: *Grey-blue fading to silver. Random silver lateral stripes.*	**Fat Content:** *Moderate–high.*
	Yield: *60% filet.*
Size: *20–40 pounds and up.*	**Available Forms:** *Steak, filet.*
Range: *Worldwide in warm oceans.*	

Frequently called the gourmet's mackerel, this delicious fish is also a sportfisherman's favorite. It occasionally comes into our markets from Hawaii, often under its local name, *ono*, which means "sweet." Its flavor is milder than that of the mackerels, to which it is related, and more like that of albacore. Use wahoo steaks or filets in place of tuna or bonito.

WHELK

(Buccinum undatum)

Other Names: *Conch, scungilli, sea snail.*	**Range:** *Different species are found from the mid-Atlantic states to Canada.*
Description: *Grey to brown snail.*	**Season:** *Spring–fall.*
	Fat Content: *Low.*
Size: *Up to 8 inches. Commonly 2 per pound.*	**Available Forms:** *Live, shucked.*

Whelk is popular in the Italian community. A Pacific Coast species can occasionally be found in Chinese markets.

Whelk is delicious when properly prepared. It has a rather tough texture, but becomes pleasantly chewy after slow cooking. Cook as for abalone after pounding, or use in Ceviche (page 70).

Whelk Vinaigrette

Serves 4 as a first course

4 whelk, in the shell
4 tablespoons olive oil
2 tablespoons lemon juice
1 teaspoon prepared mustard

2 teaspoons chopped parsley
 or other mild fresh herb
Salt and pepper to taste

Boil the whelk in lightly salted water for 3 minutes. Remove the meat from the shell. Cut the lighter-colored meat away from the soft entrails, which are not edible. Simmer for 30 minutes. Cut the meat into thin slices. Combine the remaining ingredients in a bowl large enough to hold the whelk. Add the meat to the vinaigrette, and toss thoroughly. Marinate for at least 4 hours, and preferably overnight.

Serve on a bed of lettuce or spinach, garnished with diced tomato and red onion if you like.

YELLOWTAIL

(Seriola dorsalis)

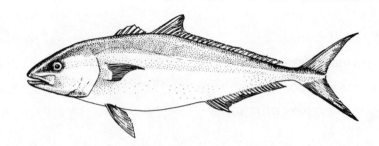

Other Names: *Yellowtail jack.*	**Season:** *Spring–summer.*
Description: *Grey-green above. Broad yellow lateral line. Silver below.*	**Fat Content:** *Moderate.*
	Yield: *60% filet.*
Size: *4–20 pounds.*	**Available Forms:** *Round, filet, steak.*
Range: *Southern California coast. Also northern Chile.*	

Yellowtail is primarily a game fish, but is occasionally available commercially. It is a member of the jack family, which includes the Florida pompano and several other popular game and food species. While less rich, it approaches tuna and wahoo in flavor and texture, and is suitable for the same cooking methods. Yellowtail is also popular for *sushi* and Sashimi (page 242), and is aquacultured in Japan.

Court-Bouillon
Poaching Liquid

Court-Bouillon is a seasoned liquid used for poaching fish, meats or vegetables. Its composition varies according to its use; the following is a fairly typical one for fish. After being used to poach fish, the liquid makes a good base for a *fumet* made with the remaining bones or trimmings.

Yield: 2 quarts

To 2 quarts water, add several sprigs of parsley or a handful of parsley stems, a few celery leaves, a bay leaf or two, 1 teaspoon cracked peppercorns, a few fennel or anise seeds or chopped fennel stalks, and a small onion, peeled and quartered, or a handful of green onion or leek tops. Adding some form of acid, either a cup of dry white wine or ¼ cup white vinegar or lemon juice, will help the fish keep its color and will absorb any ammonia flavors from shark or skate.

Bring all ingredients to a boil, simmer 20 minutes and strain.

Fumet

Fish Stock

Any part of the fish except the entrails and gills may be used to make *fumet*. Crab and shrimp shells add flavor, as do shrimp heads. Fish stocks do not need to cook nearly as long as meat stocks because the bones render their flavor quickly. Thirty minutes of cooking will produce a fairly rich stock which may then be strained and reduced.

Yield: About 3 quarts

2–3 pounds fish and shellfish
   heads, bones and
   trimmings

½ cup diced celery

2 medium yellow onions,
   peeled and diced

2 bay leaves

¼ cup parsley stems

Thyme, oregano or other
   dried herbs

Water and white wine to
   cover or Court-Bouillon
   (page 251)

Wash fish parts well. Split heads and crack large bones. Simmer all the ingredients for 30 minutes to 1 hour, skimming any foam from the surface. Strain and reserve the stock.

To freeze, pour cooled stock into a container or ice cube tray. If using a container, seal it well. Fish stock will keep 3 months in the freezer.

Beurre Blanc

This delicious and versatile sauce can be used to accompany almost any grilled, broiled or poached fish, as well as many vegetables. The reduction may be made in advance and stored, refrigerated, for several weeks. Left-over *beurre blanc* may be used as a compound butter, or may be mixed into the next batch if added very gradually.

Yield: 1 cup

¼ cup finely chopped shallots

¼ cup white wine or vermouth

¼ cup lemon juice or white wine vinegar or a mixture of the two

½ pound sweet butter, cut into cubes of 1 ounce or less

In a non-aluminum saucepan, combine the shallots and the liquids and reduce until nearly dry but not too dark. Watch carefully, as the reduction will scorch easily at this point. Remove the pan from the heat and add one or two pieces of butter. Stir steadily with a whisk or wooden spoon until the butter is melted. Return the pan to the heat and incorporate the rest of the butter, one or two pieces at a time. If the butter separates, the heat is too high; remove from the heat and stir rapidly to re-emulsify.

Serve the sauce immediately or hold it in a double boiler over barely simmering water.

Beurre Rouge

Follow the same procedure as above, using red wine and red vinegar to produce a pale rose-colored sauce which is very attractive on white-fleshed fish.

Compound Butters

Compound butters—softened butter combined with herbs, spices and other flavorings—make simple and delicious sauces for grilled, broiled or poached fish. Rolled into a cylinder in wax paper, wrapped tightly and frozen, they may be kept on hand and sliced off as needed for an instant sauce.

Maître d'Hôtel Butter

Yield: ½ cup (enough for 8 servings)

2 ounces butter, softened

1 tablespoon chopped parsley or chervil

1 teaspoon chopped shallots

¼ teaspoon lemon juice

Salt, pepper, lemon juice to taste

Beat the butter by hand or in an electric mixer until quite soft and light. Wrap the chopped herbs in a towel and squeeze out as much liquid as possible. Combine the herbs, shallots, lemon zest and butter and season to taste. Use immediately or freeze for future use; if left overnight unfrozen, the shallots will become unpleasantly strong.

Variations

Use the same procedure as above, adding salt and pepper to taste. In each case the amounts given are for 2 ounces of butter.

Anchovy Butter (*excellent on grilled shark, angler, halibut or swordfish): 1-2 anchovy filets, rinsed and chopped; zest of ½ lemon, grated and finely chopped; pinch black pepper; 1 clove garlic, blanched, peeled and pounded (optional); 1 teaspoon chopped capers (optional).*

Cilantro-Lime Butter *(goes well with strong-flavored fish such as tuna or salmon):* 2 tablespoons chopped cilantro; 1 teaspoon soy sauce; 2 teaspoons lime juice.

Wasabi Butter *(best suited to members of the tuna family and other rich fish):* 1–3 teaspoons wasabi *(page 44);* 1 teaspoon soy sauce.

Ginger-Lime Butter *(for delicate-flavored fish):* 1 teaspoon chopped or grated young ginger root; 1 teaspoon lime juice.

Hot Butter Sauces

The simplest type of sauce for grilled or broiled fish is melted butter with herbs and other seasonings added. The basic procedure is the same for all the hot butters: Melt the butter in a skillet; add the garlic or shallots and cook until they lose their raw flavor. Avoid browning the butter or overcooking the sauce, which will produce bitter or harsh flavors.

Most of the compound butters, especially those involving anchovies, may be served as hot butters as well.

The following quantities are for 2 ounces of butter, enough for 4 servings.

Basil-Garlic Butter *(use on full-flavored fish):* 1 small clove garlic, chopped or pressed; 1–2 teaspoons chopped or shredded fresh basil or *parsley* or *thyme.*

Lemon-Garlic Butter: *same as above, but substitute juice of half a lemon for basil.*

Chervil Butter *(use on delicately flavored fish):* ½ teaspoon chopped shallots; 2 teaspoons fresh chervil leaves.

Grenobloise Butter *(a classic French treatment for trout, but also delicious on grilled squid):* 1 tablespoon capers; juice of half a lemon.

Brown Butter (*good with poached skate or other poached white fish; actually a variation on Grenobloise Butter*): *cook Grenobloise Butter or butter and lemon juice until the butter browns.*

Red Hollandaise Sauce

This procedure, which can be used for Béarnaise or any other Hollandaise variation, does not involve clarified butter; the liquid from the melted butter is incorporated into the sauce in place of the water normally used to thin the sauce.

Yield: ⅔ cup

⅓ cup butter	1 tablespoon lemon juice or vinegar
½ teaspoon paprika	
Pinch cayenne (or to taste)	Salt to taste
2 egg yolks	

Melt the butter with the paprika and cayenne over low heat, without boiling. Set it aside to cool a little. When fully separated, skim off any floating solids.

In a non-aluminum double boiler or mixing bowl over hot water, beat the yolks over low heat until pale yellow and foamy. Add the lemon or vinegar and a pinch of salt, and continue beating over the heat until the mixture thickens. (Regulate the heat so the yolks do not cook too quickly. If the mixture begins to look like scrambled eggs, it is overcooked.) Remove from heat, ladle about a tablespoon of melted butter into the egg mixture, and beat until all the butter is absorbed. Add the remaining butter gradually, pouring or ladling the butterfat off the milky liquid on the bottom and beating constantly to incorporate all the butter into the sauce. If the sauce is too thick, thin it with some of the remaining liquid from the butter. Correct the seasoning.

Hollandaise may be served immediately or kept warm in a warm water bath for an hour or more.

Béarnaise Sauce

Yield: 1 cup

¼ cup white wine vinegar

¼ cup dry white wine or
  vermouth

2 teaspoons chopped shallots

2 teaspoons chopped fresh,
  or *vinegar-packed, tarragon*

⅓ cup butter

2 egg yolks

Salt and white pepper to taste

In a non-aluminum saucepan, bring the vinegar, wine, shallots and tarragon to a boil and reduce until almost all the liquid is gone. Let the mixture cool, add it to the egg yolks and proceed as for Red Hollandaise. Add more chopped tarragon to the finished sauce, if desired.

Mayonnaise

Yield: About 1½ cups

2 egg yolks

¼ teaspoon prepared mustard

¼ teaspoon salt

Pinch white pepper

1¼ cups oil (half olive and
  half peanut is a good
  blend)

3 tablespoons lemon juice
  or *white vinegar*

Have all ingredients at room temperature. If the mixing bowl is cold to the touch, warm it with hot water and dry it.

Place the egg yolks in a stainless or glass mixing bowl with the mustard, salt and pepper. Beat the mixture until pale yellow and foamy. Add a spoonful of oil and beat until it is absorbed. Continue adding oil in small quantities, beating constantly, until the mixture thickens. Once a smooth emulsion is

258   formed, the oil may be slowly poured into the bowl; however, if the sauce does not readily absorb the oil, stop adding oil and beat until smooth.

After about half of the oil has been added, alternate oil and lemon juice or vinegar. Continue until all the oil is incorporated. Correct seasoning.

Mayonnaise can also be made in a blender, food processor or tabletop mixer. Follow the same basic procedure, substituting 1 whole egg for the egg yolks if using a blender, and being careful not to add the oil too quickly.

Homemade mayonnaise will keep for several days, refrigerated and covered tightly.

Mayonnaise Variations

The following amounts are all for 1 cup of mayonnaise. The ingredients should be mixed in *after* the mayonnaise has emulsified.

Creole Mayonnaise: *Add ½ teaspoon dry mustard, ¼ teaspoon each ground white pepper, cayenne and coriander.*

Green Mayonnaise: *Add ¼ cup chopped parsley and 4 or 5 scallions blanched, cooled and finely chopped.*

Basil Mayonnaise: *Pound a handful of basil leaves in a mortar with a pinch of salt and add. (Optional: Add a clove of garlic to the basil.)*

Curry Mayonnaise: *Add ½ teaspoon or more of curry powder which has been sautéed in a small amount of oil and cooled. (This preliminary cooking prevents a bitter flavor.)*

Fines Herbes Mayonnaise: *Add 1 tablespoon or more of chopped fresh herbs—parsley, chervil, tarragon, thyme, etc.*

Jay's Tartar Sauce

1 cup Mayonnaise (page 257)

2 tablespoons chopped capers

1 tablespoon finely chopped
cornichons or gherkins

2 tablespoons finely chopped
red onion

Juice of 1 lemon

Combine and serve immediately. If the sauce is stored overnight, the onion becomes strong in flavor and makes the sauce
pink.

Isaac's Tartar Sauce

1 cup Mayonnaise (page 257)

2 teaspoons chopped garlic

1 anchovy filet, rinsed and
chopped

1 dill pickle, finely chopped

1 tablespoon chopped capers

1 tablespoon lemon juice

1 teaspoon prepared mustard

Pepper to taste

Combine all the ingredients and mix thoroughly. Serve cold or
at room temperature.

Aioli

Garlic Mayonnaise

Serve with cold poached fish, grilled fish or boiled crayfish.

Yield: About 1½ cups

3 or 4 large cloves garlic, peeled

2 egg yolks

¼ teaspoon prepared mustard

¼ teaspoon salt

Pinch white pepper

1¼ cups oil (half olive and half peanut is a good blend)

3 tablespoons lemon juice or white vinegar

Pound the garlic in a mortar to a smooth paste. Add the egg yolks and combine. Scrape this mixture into a mixing bowl and continue with the mayonnaise procedure (page 257).

Skordalia

This all-purpose almond mayonnaise is traditionally served with firm-fleshed fish such as swordfish or shark.

Yield: About 2 cups

1 cup Aioli (see above)

½ cup ground almonds

½ cup bread crumbs

2 tablespoons lemon juice

Combine and thoroughly mix all the ingredients. Serve cold or at room temperature.

Rouille

This hot garlic sauce is traditionally served with *bouillabaisse* and other fish soups. The recipe is from *The Book of Garlic* by Lloyd J. Harris.

Yield: About 1 cup

½ cup fresh bread crumbs (firmly packed)

¼ cup cold water

10 cloves garlic, finely chopped

2 teaspoons dried red pepper flakes

½ teaspoon salt

6 tablespoons olive oil

Soak the bread crumbs in water for several minutes, then squeeze dry. Pound the garlic, pepper flakes and salt to a fine paste. Add the bread crumbs and pound slowly; when they are well incorporated, stir in the oil, a tablespoon at a time. Use as much oil as is needed to make a smooth paste. The sauce should almost hold its shape in a spoon.

Parsley Sauce

For grilled mild fish.

Yield: About ¾ cup

2 teaspoons chopped garlic

¼ cup finely chopped parsley

¼ cup bread crumbs

1 hard-boiled egg

6 black olives, pitted

¼ cup or more olive oil

Salt and pepper to taste

Purée all the ingredients in a blender or food processor until smooth. Serve immediately or refrigerate and serve chilled. This sauce will keep 3–4 days.

Tarator Sauce

This is not related to tartar sauce, despite the similar name.
Serve with fried shellfish or grilled fish.

Yield: About 1 cup

¼ cup bread crumbs

¼ cup walnuts

1 tablespoon minced garlic

2 tablespoons lemon juice

2 tablespoons white vinegar

⅜ cup olive oil

Salt and pepper to taste

Blend all the ingredients until smooth in a food processor or
blender. If making the sauce by hand, chop the nuts finely, and
combine all the ingredients in a bowl; beat until smooth.

Fresh Tomato Salsa

Yield: 1 cup

1 large tomato, peeled,
  seeded and diced

¼ cup chopped scallions
  or mild onion

1 or 2 serrano or other small
  hot chiles, seeded and
  finely chopped

2 tablespoons chopped
  cilantro

Salt to taste

Combine all ingredients at least an hour before serving to allow
flavors to marry. If more chile flavor is desired, add more seeded
and chopped chiles. For a hotter sauce, the seeds and veins of
the chiles may be included.

Leftover *salsa* will not have the crisp texture of the fresh sauce, but may be used in hot dishes or heated in butter for grilled crab or other shellfish.

Sauce Mignonette

Yield: Enough for 24 oysters served on the half-shell

1 shallot, finely chopped
2 teaspoons dry white wine

Red wine vinegar and black pepper to taste

Combine all the ingredients. Serve at room temperature.

Soy-Sesame Dipping Sauce

This is a dipping sauce for boiled or steamed crab, or grilled mild fish.

Yield: About ½ cup

¼ cup red wine vinegar
2 tablespoons soy sauce
2 teaspoons chopped ginger

1 teaspoon sesame oil
1 teaspoon sugar

Combine all the ingredients and mix thoroughly. Serve at room temperature.

Teriyaki Sauce

This recipe first appeared in Isaac's *International Squid Cookbook*.

Yield: 1½ cups

½ cup medium soy sauce	2 tablespoons lemon juice
½ cup mirin or ½ cup dry sherry	1 teaspoon cornstarch dissolved in 1 tablespoon water
½ cup water	

To use as a marinade, combine all the ingredients except for the cornstarch.

To make a basting sauce, heat the marinade until it boils and then add the cornstarch mixture. When the sauce thickens, remove it from the heat and let it cool slightly.

Green Chile Sauce

Somchai Aksomboon

This spicy mixture from Thailand is delicious with any grilled fish or shellfish.

Yield: About ½ cup

2 ounces jalapeño or *other* medium-hot chiles, chopped	2 tablespoons chopped cilantro root
¼ cup plain distilled vinegar	1 tablespoon chopped garlic
	Salt to taste

Pureé all the ingredients in a blender or food processor. Serve at room temperature or chilled. This sauce does not keep well.

Fresh Cilantro Chutney

This easy-to-prepare chutney is a fine condiment for grilled or broiled fish. It is best eaten fresh, but will keep refrigerated for a day or so.

Yield: About ½ cup

1 cup cilantro

4 scallions, roughly chopped

1 tablespoon lemon juice

2 small hot green chiles

1 teaspoon garam masala (page 40), or ¼ teaspoon each ground turmeric, cinnamon, cloves and cumin

Blend all the ingredients in a blender or food processor until smooth, adding a tiny amount of water if necessary to make a smooth paste.

Red Curry Paste

This spicy paste is the basis for a number of Thai curries, usually in conjunction with coconut milk (page 39) and fish sauce (page 40). It will keep for 3–4 days in the refrigerator.

Yield: ¼ cup

5 dried red chiles, seeded, soaked in water and then drained

Salt and pepper to taste

2 teaspoons ground caraway seeds

2 teaspoons ground coriander seeds

1 teaspoon coriander root

2 teaspoons finely chopped fresh lemongrass or 1 teaspoon chopped dried lemongrass

1 teaspoon finely chopped Laos root (page 41)

1 tablespoon chopped shallots

½ teaspoon shrimp paste (optional) (page 43)

Pound all the ingredients together in a mortar, or blend them in a food processor. The paste should be as smooth as possible.

Wood-burning pizza ovens are turning out to be to the early eighties what charcoal grilling was to the late seventies—the latest rediscovered cooking technique. While home ovens cannot match the heat of such specialized equipment, baking pizza on an unglazed earthenware surface can produce nearly the same result. Some cookware shops are carrying special round "pizza tiles," but a cheaper solution is available in the form of terra cotta quarry tiles, about 12 inches square, available at building supply yards.

The following recipe gives the general procedure for seafood pizza and a few suggestions for topping combinations. Note that none of these calls for cooked tomato sauce, which can easily overwhelm the other ingredients.

Pizza Dough

Yield: Four 11-inch pizzas or 4 calzones

1 package (1 tablespoon)
  baker's yeast

1½ cups warm (100°) water

4 cups unbleached bread or
  all-purpose flour

1 tablespoon olive oil

Rice flour, unbleached bread
  or all-purpose flour or
  cornmeal

Olive oil

Dissolve the yeast and 1 tablespoon of flour in ¼ cup of the water. Make sure the yeast bubbles, indicating it is active. Set the yeast aside for 10–15 minutes. Pour the rest of the flour into a bowl. Add the yeast liquid and a little of the water. Stir with a large spoon. Add the rest of the liquid and the olive oil and mix thoroughly, using your hands. This whole procedure can be accomplished quickly in a food processor, using the plastic dough blade. Knead the dough by hand or by machine until it is smooth and resilient. Form into a ball. Oil the bottom of a bowl, and place the dough in it. Cover with a damp towel. Let it rise until it doubles in size, about 2 hours. Punch the dough down and divide into 4 pieces.

Making the Pizza Crust

Form each piece of dough into a ball. Roll each ball on the pastry board with one hand until the top surface is smooth. Place them on a tray at least 2 inches apart, cover with a damp towel and let them rest at least 30 minutes and up to 3–4 hours. (Dough may be prepared to this point and refrigerated overnight; allow at least 1 hour for the dough to warm up to room temperature before forming the pizzas.)

To form pizzas by hand: Dust the board lightly with rice flour, unbleached bread, all purpose flour or cornmeal. With the fingertips, press the dough into a circle of equal thickness, about 6 inches in diameter. Pick up the circle between the palms and fingers of both hands and gently stretch the edge of the circle. Work around the edge, letting the dough hang. As the dough stretches to about 8 or 9 inches in diameter, drape it over the back of one hand and wrist and stretch with the other hand. Continue working around the circle until the dough is about 11 inches across.

With a rolling pin: If the above procedure is too difficult to follow, the dough may be rolled out into an 11-inch circle with a rolling pin. The crust will, however, have a heavier texture than a hand-formed pizza.

Place the dough on a baking sheet sprinkled with cornmeal or, if baking directly on a tile surface, on the *underside* of a baking sheet sprinkled with cornmeal. If there are any holes or very thin spots in the dough, stretch enough from a thicker spot to close them. Compress or roll the edge of the dough slightly, forming a raised rim. Brush the dough lightly with a little olive oil, the best possible quality. Sprinkle with chopped garlic and the remaining toppings, such as those suggested below. If baking on tiles, gently slide the pizza onto the tiles, taking care not to dislodge the toppings or tear the dough. Bake until the edge of the dough is golden brown. With a wide spatula or two, transfer the pizza to a serving platter or a cutting board which can go to the table. Sprinkle with a bit more olive oil and fresh herbs, if desired.

Pizza Toppings

The following are some suggested combinations, each listed in recommended order of assembly. Most contain at least one salty ingredient, so additional salt will not be needed, but black pepper should be added to taste.

Yield: Enough for 11-inch pizza

Shrimp and Feta: *½ cup peeled, seeded and sliced tomato, ¼ cup crumbled feta cheese, fresh oregano or marjoram, 4–6 ounces peeled small shrimp.*

Clam and Mussel: *½ cup grated Parmesan or Romano cheese, ¼–½ pound steamed and shucked clams or mussels, extra garlic, chopped parsley.*

Tuna with Fresh Herbs: *½ cup tomato, 4–6 ounces fresh tuna, bonito or squid in ¾-inch cubes, 2–4 anchovy filets (rinsed and coarsely chopped), fresh thyme, marjoram or oregano.*

Mixed Shellfish Calzone

Calzone, a sort of pizza turnover originally from Florence, is becoming very popular in many of the newer upscale pizzerias. The classic version contains only cheeses, herbs and *prosciutto* or *pancetta*; the addition of tomatoes is considered heresy in Florence, but is fairly common here. Our version uses a typical cheese mixture, an atypical assortment of seafood, and no tomato.

Serves 2

⅓ cup grated mozzarella cheese

⅓ cup ricotta cheese

¼ cup grated Parmesan cheese

½ teaspoon chopped garlic

1 tablespoon chopped parsley

Salt and pepper to taste

½ cup assorted shellfish: steamed and shucked mussels or clams; shucked and drained oysters; peeled shrimp, roughly chopped if large; and squid, cut into rings and blanched

¼ recipe Pizza Dough (see above)

Combine the cheeses, garlic and parsley and season to taste. Add the shellfish and set aside. Preheat oven to 500°.

Lightly dust the pastry board with rice flour or all-purpose flour. Roll the dough out to a 12-inch circle. Place the cheese mixture on one side of the dough, leaving at least a 2-inch margin. Brush the edge of the dough with a little water and fold the other half of the dough over the filling, matching the edges. Fold the sealed edge inward in a decorative pattern. Bake on tiles or a baking sheet until crust is golden brown and sounds hollow when tapped. Brush the top with olive oil and sprinkle with Parmesan, if desired. Serve with knives and forks.

(Note: Smaller, individual calzones may be made, but will require proportionately more dough.)

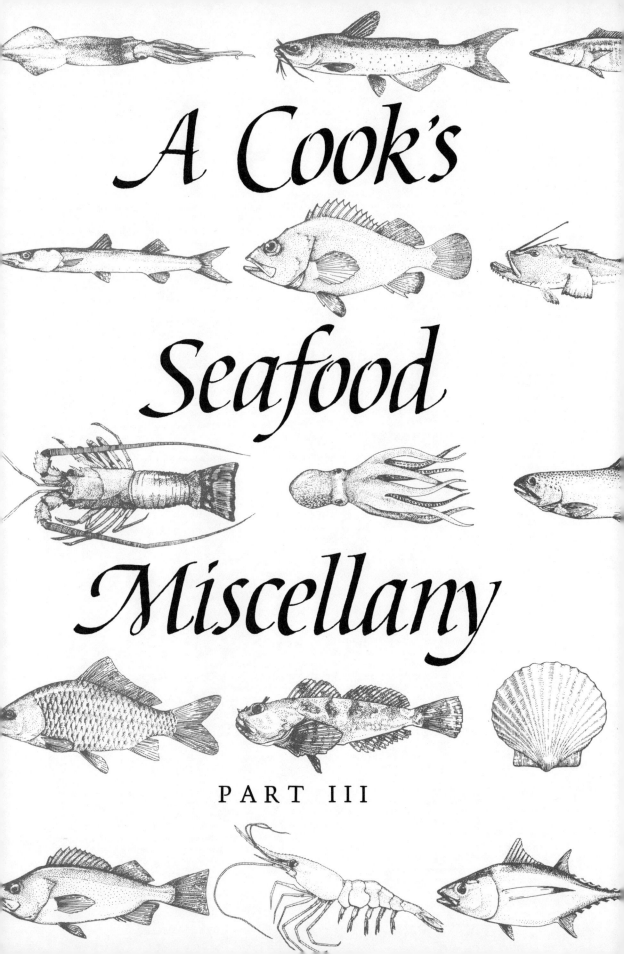

A Cook's

Seafood

Miscellany

PART III

A FISHMONGER'S DAY

(Editor's Note: The following is an account of a typical day for Paul Johnson and those who work with him. Paul is a whole-sale and retail fish dealer in daily contact with all facets of the seafood business. As is true for many of his colleagues, his concern for quality and freshness is evidenced by the rigors and challenges of his day. For all his success, Paul is very modest and resisted the inclusion of this portrait. The editor, however, prevailed.)

*P*AUL wakes up at 3:15 am. As he drives from the East Bay and through San Francisco, he passes newspapermen, garbage collectors and a few transients sleeping in doorways. Otherwise, the streets are empty.

At 4, give or take ten minutes, Paul arrives at the wharf in San Francisco. On any given day, where he stops first depends on which wholesalers have boats out fishing and on what kind of fish they are likely to catch. Today, the first call is on Standard Fish. He buys 400 pounds of rockfish, including fantails, boccacios, yellowtail and blacks. There is no time to check the quality of each fish, but Paul knows how they were caught and when the boats arrived, and makes his selections based on that information. He will return to this dealer later in the morning, so he reports his weights and leaves without signing the bill.

By 4:30, the wharf is bustling with activity. The distributors and their crews are hard at work unloading and moving fish, shoveling ice and filling orders. Paul comes to the wharf five days a week; one of his assistants does the buying on a sixth. He knows the buyers and sellers and they all know him. Their business dealings follow a strict but unwritten code which it has taken Paul awhile to learn. His experience and his reputation as a consistent, steady customer for large quantities of fresh seafood enable him to obtain quality seafood every day.

Paul knows that two boats fishing for two different companies are due to arrive at 4:30. He makes an educated guess as to which one will have the fish he needs—in this case the rather scarce halibut—and drives along the Embarcadero to the docks. Today, he has guessed right. Hayes Street Grill will be pleased with the 150 pounds of large halibut.

Fifteen minutes later he drives back to the wharf and stops at another wholesaler. He buys another 400 pounds of rockfish, which he will filet a few hours later in his shop in Berkeley. Paul exchanges wharf gossip and information as he waits in line for a bill. As he leaves, Paul is approached by another wholesaler who has arrived a few minutes late, missed all his connections and ended up empty-handed. Paul sells him some of the halibut which he hustled to find, knowing the favor will be returned.

As he hands over the fish, Paul learns that a drag boat has just docked with a good catch. Losing no time, he walks over to the end of the wharf. A crowd of wholesalers has already gathered. This is winter and fish are somewhat scarce. Paul quickly sizes things up and places his order. He buys 500 pounds of the prized petrale sole, 150 pounds of rex sole, and 250 pounds of lingcod.

A few minutes before 7:00, Paul picks up a 250-pound crate of crabs which had been delivered after Paul left the wharf the day before. (Having learned yesterday that there would be no fresh crabs today, he phoned ahead to have some set aside. They are waiting for him in a covered box, stored in the ocean.) The van is nearly full now with more than a ton of fish.

Earlier, Paul had looked for the California Seafood Express, a daily express truck delivery from San Pedro. He has 470 pounds of Hawaiian tuna on order but today he will have to do without. The driver, seeing the name "Monterey Fish" on the box, thought Paul's tuna belonged in Monterey, which is where he left them. Paul has to make substitutions; there is no time to fret over mistakes. Fortunately, another wholesaler hears of his plight and offers him some wahoo which have not yet been claimed.

Just before 8:00, Paul leaves San Francisco, crossing the Bay Bridge against the rush-hour traffic. When he arrives at the shop, he and his staff, who opened up an hour earlier, unload the fish and begin fileting and sorting. While Peter and Jed cut,

Paul is on the phone to his suppliers. He calls San Pedro to en-
quire about his tuna and to request mackerel, squid (fresh from
Southern California during the winter months) and bonito for
tomorrow. Another call, this time to Washington state for
steelhead and geoduck clams. Then he phones a San Francisco
broker who will arrange for the shipment of scallops, mussels
and angler from the East Coast. Finally, Paul speaks to an
Hawaiian broker who will send him more tuna, mahi-mahi and
spearfish.

Around 9:00, the restaurants begin to call in. Each of Paul's
restaurant accounts orders daily, selecting from a list patiently
recited for each customer. Some have called in requests the
night before on his answering machine. Paul has dealt with
most of his customers for years and knows their likes and dis-
likes, so he has bought accordingly. Most of them serve a variety
of fresh seafood, listing their daily selection on a chalkboard or
a clip-on list attached to their menus. The orders are quickly
assembled by Joan and Robert, as much of the fish is needed for
lunch.

By 10:30, Peter leaves with the San Francisco deliveries, and
Jed heads for the East Bay restaurants with the other truck.
After delivering fish to the Hayes Street Grill, Balboa Cafe,
Zuni Cafe and Squid's, Peter heads for San Francisco Airport to
pick up 400 pounds of steelhead which have just arrived by air
from Washington. Jed makes the rounds to Chez Panisse, the
Fourth Street Grill, Santa Fe Bar and Grill, Augusta's and Bay
Wolf, then returns to the shop to assemble other orders for
dinner.

Paul, Jed and Peter spend the early afternoon filling dinner
orders and making additional pick-ups at the airport and other
deliveries wherever they are needed. Paul tries to finish his day
by 3:00, but sometimes he works much later. With luck, he
will get to bed by 8:00 so he can rise at 3:15 to begin his day
again.

WINE AND SEAFOOD

*A*LONG with the dramatic increases in the quality and worldwide reputation of California wines has come a steady increase in the sophistication of the American wine drinker. Many are learning to trust their own tastes more than the oversimplifications of traditional wine and food affinity charts. It no longer seems heretical to suggest, for example, that some red wines be served with fish.

Of course, the traditional combination of dry white wines and seafood is still valid. But many of the attributes of the classic seafood wines apply equally to certain red wines: good acidity, little or no tannin, light to medium body and not-too-pronounced varietal character. Conversely, a big, powerful oak-aged white wine (including many of California's most celebrated wines) may be too much for simple seafood dishes.

Rather than suggesting specific wines to go with each recipe in this book, we offer the following guidelines. Limitations of space prevent us from mentioning many other suitable wines.

One classic combination with which we cannot argue is *oysters and Champagne.* Chablis (the real thing from Chablis, not the ubiquitous domestic version) and Côteaux Champenois (basically Champagne without the bubbles) are also excellent choices, and Muscadet is a more than adequate alternative. All are bone dry with good acidity and a characteristic soil flavor which goes nicely with the rich texture and fresh seawater flavor of the oysters.

For most simple preparations of *grilled, poached or broiled fish,* choose a dry white of light to medium body. If there is an all-purpose seafood wine, it may be Sancerre, which has a definite Sauvignon Blanc character in delightful harmony with the local soil. Other choices would be lighter California Chardonnay or Sauvignon Blanc, dry Chenin Blanc or French Colombard; Mâcon or other light white Burgundy, Pouilly-Fumé, white Bordeaux, Muscadet or Alsatian Riesling; or various Italian whites such as the Pinot Bianco or Pinot Grigio of the Northeast or Gavi from Piedmont.

For richer fish and shellfish, especially when prepared with cream, some of the bigger whites, California Chardonnays and whites from the Côte de Beaune in particular, should be added to the above list in place of some of the lighter wines.

Fish with a pronounced flavor, such as tuna, and preparations with such Mediterranean flavors as anchovy, garlic and olives, are better served by a fuller-bodied white, blanc de noirs, rosé or a light red. With these dishes, try some of the following: whites and rosés from the Rhône and Provence or from southern Italy; slightly chilled Beaujolais, red Côtes du Rhône, Chianti, Valpolicella or California Gamay; or "white" wines made from red grapes, especially Pinot Noir, which are labeled under a variety of names such as Pinot Noir Blanc and Vin Gris.

Latin American, Southeast Asian, Chinese and Creole cuisines are harder to match with wines. For milder dishes, follow the above guidelines. A white wine with a very pronounced aroma and flavor, such as Gewürztraminer, is frequently suggested with such flavors as pepper, ginger and garlic; some experts suggest Sancerre or another Sauvignon instead. (Another expert, wine importer and writer Gerald Asher, has suggested a different approach to wine and Chinese food. The array of flavors and textures in a Chinese meal, he says, is only confused by the addition of an assertive wine. He recommends instead a mild, off-dry wine such as a Chenin Blanc, to serve as a "silk curtain" behind the food.) Where fresh or dried chiles are a major ingredient in a dish, no wine will be complemented by the food, and the wine is mainly a refreshment. A little sweetness goes a long way in softening the effect of hot pepper on the palate, so an off-dry to slightly sweet wine might be in order. For really hot dishes, however, the best beverage is beer.

Riesling seems especially well suited to *freshwater fish*. Several German producers are once again shipping dry or nearly-dry wines in addition to the better-known sweet wines. Look for the word "Trocken" or "Halbtroken" on the main label or neck label. Try these with trout, steelhead or salmon.

If wine is used in any quantity in a dish, serve the same or the same type of wine.

THE CALIFORNIA OYSTER STORY

*T*HE oyster has an exotic reputation in almost every culture where it is a food. Its reputation as an aphrodisiac is legendary and often overshadows the oyster's culinary virtues. For now we will leave aside its effects on human sexual behavior to consider the no less interesting story of the oyster's own reproductive life.

California oyster aquaculture began in the first days of the Gold Rush. Oysters were a delicacy much in demand in the strike-it-rich atmosphere of the mining camps. Local supplies of the indigenous Pacific oyster were quickly exhausted by the huge demand. The cry for oysters was so loud that Eastern oysters were dispatched by boat around South America, and small Pacific oysters were sent from Oregon and Washington to be transplanted in the San Francisco Bay to mature.

Completion of the transcontinental railroad encouraged the shipment of small Eastern oysters to the West Coast and they, too, were grown to full size in the Bay. However, they never reproduced here and eventually that part of the industry died out.

As the water quality of the Bay deteriorated, all "grow-out" activity declined, and by 1939 the San Francisco Bay oyster industry disappeared.

In the early 1930s, Japanese oyster seed was brought to the Pacific coast. The Japanese oyster was ideally suited to the region and has flourished despite a period of decline during the 1940s and early 1950s. Today, the Japanese oyster is the single most important species in California. It is grown primarily in Humboldt, Drake's, Tomales and Morro bays. The French Belon oyster was introduced to California seven years ago and it does quite well here too; in fact, Belon seed is now exported back to France.

Oyster Aquaculture

There are two methods for growing oysters, known in the trade as *cultch* and *cultchless*.

Cultch Method

In the *cultch* method there are two different techniques. In one, more common in Pacific bays, the fertilized eggs are spread on strings of oyster shells suspended in the water; the strings are hauled out of the water for harvest and re-seeded. The other, termed the broadcast technique, is more common in Eastern and Gulf coast oyster beds. The fertilized eggs are spread (broadcast) over the beds of shells; the oysters are harvested by dredging, after which the beds are rebuilt and re-seeded. Since string culture uses more of the water's depth than broadcasting, it allows more yield per acre.

Cultchless Method

In the cultchless method, each fertilized egg attaches itself to a tiny piece of ground shell. The process begins in the laboratory under carefully controlled conditions. Separate tanks of male and female oysters are induced by warm water to spawn; the eggs are then fertilized by hand. The fertilized eggs are poured into tanks containing warm filtered seawater and fed a diet of cultured microscopic algae.

After a few weeks of steady growth they are poured through screens. The biggest oysters are caught and the smaller (and slower growing) ones fall through to be discarded. This sizing process, which is repeated every few days, produces a uniformly sturdy stock with a high survival rate. Growth and screening continue for two weeks. Finely chopped shell is then introduced and the oysters grow a foot which attaches to the small pieces in the same way that cultch oysters attach to strings or beds of shells. At this stage, oysters are known as "spat." Selective screening continues until the spat reach a size of 2–3 mm. Oyster spat can be packed into small boxes—a tiny crate will hold thousands—and shipped any place in the world where water conditions are suitable for grow-out. The survival rate of properly handled spat is well above 50%.

In the "nursery stage," the spat are floated in salt bays in boxes covered with fine mesh, washed and sometimes screened. The oysters are transferred to various containers to mature: nets suspended from rafts; bags suspended on racks extending above the bottom of the bay; or bags resting on the bottom. The oysters mature in 9–10 months, then are removed, washed and packed for immediate shipping, or held for later use in tanks containing purified seawater.

This approach, which was perfected in the 1960s, allows for quicker and more uniform growth and a higher survival rate than the cultch. The oysters also tend to be leaner and more flavorful.

AN OUNCE OF PREVENTION

W HILE seafood is widely and rightly viewed as health-
ful food, there are a few health risks associated with
fish and shellfish. These include toxins inherent in
the fish, toxins produced by other organsms, and parasites. Fortunately these dangers are relatively rare, and high-risk situations are easily identifiable.

Two fish that have *poisonous roe* are commonly eaten by
Americans: cabezon (a Pacific coast sculpin) and alligator gar (a
large Gulf coast species). The flesh is perfectly safe; only the
eggs should be avoided.

Certain freshwater or anadramous species such as salmon are
occasionally infested with a *tapeworm* (*Diphllobothrium* sp.)
which is contracted during their freshwater cycle. These
worms, which parasitize humans as well as animals, are easy to
avoid. Either eat only anadramous fish caught in the open sea,
or follow the precautions suggested by the National Center for
Disease Control:

> Fish tapeworm infection . . . can be prevented by cooking until
> all parts of the fish reach a temperature of at least 113° for five
> minutes. Freezing to 0° farenheit for 24 hours can also prevent
> infection. Preparation by placing the fish in a brine solution
> may be effective if appropriate salt concentration, filet size
> and contact time are observed. Commercially prepared lox is
> usually brined before smoking and should not constitute a
> source of infection.

Tapeworms can cause extremely unpleasant symptoms and
precautionary measures should be taken. Freshwater and anadramous fish which have not first been frozen are not recommended for *sashimi, ceviche* or any other uncooked preparation.

Certain fish species, notably mahi-mahi and tuna, contain
large quantities of an amino acid called histidine which con-
verts to histamines after the fish is caught. If the fish is not properly iced, as is sometimes the case in tropical fishing grounds,
histamine production is accelerated. Individual sensitivity to
histimine varies, and in some people these fish may produce
histamine poisoning. Symptoms commonly include flushing,

282   headache, dizziness, thick tongue and heaviness in the chest. The symptoms come on quickly, much like an MSG reaction, although they are more severe and last longer. Histamine poisoning is routinely treated with antihistamines; after proper care the ill effects disappear quickly.

The most serious threat to health is also the best known—*shellfish poisoning*. Shellfish poisoning is the result of a one-celled organism, a *dynoflagellate* called *Gonyaulax catenella*, which "blooms" only in temperate waters during the summer months. There is an official quarantine on all wild bivalves in California from May 1 to October 31. During that period it is unsafe to eat mussels, oysters or clams; these bivalves are filter-feeders which ingest *dynoflagellates* in large quantities and concentrate the toxin in the dark portions of their meat. Harvesting of commercial oyster beds is carefully monitored by the Federal Trade Commission for *dynoflagellate* levels during summer months. Harvesting is halted whenever there is a significant risk. Fresh aquacultured oysters are therefore available through most of the summer. Shellfish poisoning can be fatal. The toxin is not destroyed by freezing, cooking or aging, and there is no simple way to determine whether a particular bivalve is toxic before you eat it.

BIBLIOGRAPHY

Davidson, Alan, *Mediterranean Seafood*, Louisiana State University Press, Baton Rouge, Louisiana, 1972.

Davidson, Alan, *North Atlantic Seafood*, Viking Press, N.Y., 1979.

Gates, Doyle and Frey, Herbert, "Designated Common Names of Certain Marine Organisms of California," California Department of Fish and Game, Sacramento, California, 1972.

Johnson, Myrtle and Snook, Harry, *Seashore Animals of the Pacific Coast*, Dover Publications, N.Y., 1927.

Miller, Daniel and Lea, Robert, *Guide to the Coastal Marine Fishes of California*, California Department of Fish and Game, Sacramento, California, 1972.

McClane, A.J., *The Encyclopedia of Fish Cookery*, Holt, Rinehart and Winston, N.Y., 1977.

McClane, A.J. (Ed.), *Field Guide to Freshwater Fishes of North America*, Holt, Rinehart and Winston, N.Y., 1965.

McClane, A.J. (Ed.) *Field Guide to Saltwater Fishes of North America*, Holt, Rinehart and Winston, N.Y., 1965.

Index

Italic page numbers refer to the encyclopedic entries for each species. Other references to a given species (as an alternative or in passing) follow in Roman type. Recipes are listed in boldface.

About the Authors and Illustrator

Isaac Cronin has written numerous magazine articles on food as well as several cookbooks, including *The International Squid Cookbook* and *Eating For Two: The Complete Pregnancy Nutrition Cookbook.*

Jay Harlow has worked as a chef at several fine Bay Area seafood restaurants. He is currently administrative director of the American Institute of Wine and Food in San Francisco.

Paul Johnson operates Monterey Fish in Berkeley, California, suppliers of seafood to many of the finest restaurants in the Bay Area.

Amy Pertschuk is the scientific illustrator for the Ichthyology Department at The California Academy of Sciences in San Francisco.

Cookbooks from Aris Books

The Book of Garlic by Lloyd J. Harris. The book that started America's love affair with garlic. It consolidates recipes, lore, history, medicinal concoctions and much more. "Admirably researched and well written."—Craig Claiborne in *The New York Times*. Third, revised edition: 286 pages, paper $9.95

The International Squid Cookbook by Isaac Cronin. A charming collection of recipes, curiosities and culinary information. "A culinary myopia for squid lovers."— *New York Magazine*. 96 pages, paper $6.95

Mythology and Meatballs: A Greek Island Diary/Cookbook by Daniel Spoerri. A marvelous, magical travel/gastronomic diary with fascinating recipes, anecdotes, mythologies and much more. ". . . a work to be savored in the reading . . ." —*Newsweek*. 238 pages, cloth $14.95

The Feast of the Olive: Cooking with Olives and Olive Oil by Maggie Blyth Klein. A complete recipe and reference guide to using fine olive oils and a variety of cured olives. 175 pages, cloth $16.95, paper $9.95

The Art of Filo Cookbook: International Entrees, Appetizers & Desserts Wrapped in Flaky Pastry by Marti Sousanis. At long last, a comprehensive guide to making filo pastries at home. 144 pages, paper $8.95

To receive the above titles, send a check or money order made out to Aris Books for the amount of the book plus $1.75 postage and handling for the first title, and 75¢ for each additional title. To receive our current catalogue of new titles, send your name and address plus 50¢ for postage and handling.

Aris Books, 1635 Channing Way, Berkeley, CA 94703   (415) 843-0330